TYNDALE is a registered trademark of Tyndale House Publishers, Inc.

Tyndale Kids logo is a trademark of Tyndale House Publishers, Inc.

Eager Reader Bible

Copyright © 1994 by Tyndale House Publishers, Inc. All rights reserved.

Produced by Educational Publishing Concepts

Text by Daryl J. Lucas of the Livingstone Corporation
Livingstone Project Staff: Betsy Elliot, Jim Galvin, Dave Veerman

Cover designed by Jacqueline L. Noe

For manufacturing information regarding this product, please call
1-800-323-9400.

ISBN 978-0-8423-1338-4

Printed in China

14 13 12 11 10
13 12 11 10 9

The Eager Reader

BIBLE

Bible Stories to Grow On

Eager Reader
BIBLE

Bible Stories to Grow On

Daryl J. Lucas

Illustrated by Daniel J. Hochstatter

TYNDALE KiDS

Tyndale House Publishers, Inc., Carol Stream, Illinois

Note to Parents

The Bible tells us, "Bring up children in the way they should go, and when they are old they will not depart from it." Another way to say this is, "By the time a child is six years old, much of his or her character has been shaped for life."

So what an awesome time these few swiftly passing years are for parents. How can we as parents improve those shining hours of opportunity?

Many parents choose a special time for reading together as a family. A public school-teacher I recently talked with told me that children who are read to at home are usually the best students at school. On the contrary, children who spend a couple of hours a day watching TV are less attentive, easily distracted, and often lack emotional stability. Doubtless the togetherness of parents and children is as important as the reading itself.

I recommend an after-supper (or after-school) reading time as one of the best ways for parents and children to spend time together. This will require frequent trips to the church and public library, and must surely include Bible storybooks like this one as well as stories read as early as possible directly from the Bible.

When we read Bible stories with our children, we instill the timeless values and life-lessons of the Scriptures. We introduce them to its important people and themes. Above all, we introduce them to God and to his Son, Jesus. Reading Bible stories with your children will plant seeds that will grow throughout their lifetime.

This book, and others like it, will build faith in God and give an enormous head start in understanding and trusting him throughout the pathway ahead. It will help guide little feet into the way of Life.

Kenneth N. Taylor

CONTENTS

God Made Everything

In the beginning, there was nothing. So God made the world.

Then God said, "Let there be light!" And there was light.

But the earth was empty. So God said, "Let there be sky!" And a blue sky appeared.

And God said, "Let there be land and seas, and plants to live there!" And it was so.

Genesis 1–2

But the night sky was still dark. So God said, "Let the moon and stars appear!" And soon the night sky shone with their light.

But the earth still had no animals of any kind. So God said, "Let there be birds and fish!" And soon birds flew and fish swam.

 What did God make first?

But the land had no creatures. So God said, "Let the land have animals too!" And all kinds of animals came to life.

God looked at all he had made and smiled. He was glad he had made the sky, the land, the seas, the plants, the stars, the moon, the birds, the fish, and the land animals. It was all good.

But there was still no one to rule the earth. So God took some dirt and made it into a man. God gave the man life. And God named him Adam. Then God made a woman from Adam's rib, and Adam named her Eve.

When God was done, he had made everything– the sky, the land, the moon and stars, the seas, the plants, the animals, and people.

And all of it was very good.

 What did God make last?

The Very First Sin

Adam and Eve lived in a beautiful and perfect garden called Eden. They were happy there. They had everything they needed.

But one day Satan came to the Garden. He didn't want Adam and Eve to be happy. So he disguised himself as a tricky snake.

Genesis 3

The snake went up to Eve. "Did God tell you not to eat the fruit in the Garden?" he asked.

"No," said Eve. "We may eat from any tree except one. If we eat from that tree, we will die."

"That's silly!" the snake hissed. "You won't die. If you eat that fruit, you will know as much as God does."

 Who was the snake?

Hmmm, thought Eve. *The fruit does look pretty. And it would be wonderful to know as much as God does.*

Eve reached for a piece of the fruit and took a bite. Then she gave some to her husband, Adam. He ate it too.

Right away they knew they had done something wrong. God had said not to eat the fruit. But they did.

Adam and Eve tried to hide from God, but God found them. "Why did you eat the fruit I said not to eat?" God asked.

"The snake tricked me," Eve answered.

"Eve gave it to me," Adam said.

God was very sad. Now Adam and Eve would grow old and die. They would have to leave Eden forever.

 What did Adam and Eve do wrong?

Noah Builds a Boat

Adam and Eve had many children. These children grew up, got married, and had many more children. Before long the earth was full of people.

But almost all of the people were very bad. They hurt each other a lot. All they could think about was how to do bad things.

God was very sad. He didn't want all the evil to go on. So God decided to flood the whole earth.

Noah loved God. He was the only good man in the whole world. God didn't want Noah and his family to get punished. They would need protection from the big flood.

"Noah," said God, "build a huge boat!"

 Why did God want to flood the earth?

"OK, Lord," said Noah.

Noah and his family worked and worked. They chopped down trees. They made boards. They put the boards together.

Once the boat took shape, they covered it with tar so the water couldn't get in. The boat was called an ark.

Finally, when Noah and his family finished the ark, Noah's family and many, many animals would fit inside. The ark was huge!

 What did Noah use to build the ark?

The Big Flood

It took a long time for Noah and his family to finish the ark. But finally they did.

"It's going to rain soon," God said. "Now gather two of every kind of animal. Take them all with you on the ark."

Noah gathered the animals just as God said. Then he and his family went into the ark, and God shut the door.

The rain started to pour down.

Genesis 6–9

It rained hard and long. Puddles turned into lakes. Everywhere the earth started to flood. But Noah's ark floated! The water rose higher and higher. After forty days and nights, everything everywhere was under water.

Then the rain stopped.

 How long did it rain?

Everyone in the whole world drowned except
the people and animals on the ark.

It took a long time for the water to go down. So
Noah and his family waited. The ark came to rest on
top of a mountain. As soon as the water dried up,
Noah opened the door. People and animals ran out.

"Thank you, God!" said Noah.

God was happy to hear Noah's praise. He promised never to flood the earth again. He set a rainbow in the sky to remind people of his promise.

"Never again will I destroy the earth like that," God said. And God always keeps his promises.

What was God's promise?

God Speaks to Abram and Sarai

Many years passed after the big flood. But God didn't forget about the world.

There was a man named Abram. He believed in God. So did his wife. She was named Sarai. They were old and had no children.

But God had a wonderful plan for them.

God said, "Abram, I want you to go to a new land. I am going to make you great. One day you and Sarai will have a child. Your child will have a family too. Someday, your family will fill up a whole country!

"Now go! I will show you where to live."

What did God want Abram to do?

Abram and Sarai packed up all their things.
They put everything on donkeys and camels.

Their nephew Lot went with them. So did all
their workers.

They walked and walked for hundreds of miles.
God showed them the way.

Finally, they came to a land they had never seen before. It was called Canaan. God said, "This is your land, Abram!"

So Abram and Sarai set up their tents and worshiped God.

 What was Abram's new land called?

Abram and Lot

Abram and Sarai had many animals and tents. They were very rich.

Their nephew Lot also had many animals and tents. But all of them lived on the same land.

Lot's workers argued with Abram's workers. "You're taking our space!" they yelled. "No," the others answered. "YOU'RE taking OUR space!"

Genesis 13

So Abram said, "Let's not fight. We are family. If we spread out, we will have plenty of room. You take whatever land you want. I'll take what's left over."

Lot looked around. The valley had lots of green grass. It had streams and ponds. "I'll take that part," said Lot.

 What nice thing did Abram do?

35

So Lot took the best land for himself. He moved to the nice green valley. Abram stayed in the hills.

Then God spoke to Abram. "Look all around you—north, south, east, and west. See all this land? One day you, your children, and your grandchildren will own all of it. Your family will be like grains of sand on a beach—too many to count."

Abram hiked all over his new land. He decided to live near Hebron, where big oak trees grew. Abram and Sarai set up their tents. And Abram built an altar so they could worship God.

 What did Abram do in his new land?

Lot Escapes a Fire

Lot lived in a town called Sodom. One evening two men came to Sodom. Lot met them at the gate. "Come to my house," Lot said.

(The visitors were really angels, but Lot didn't know it.)

The polite visitors said no. But Lot said, "Please come." So they did.

They ate dinner together.

Genesis 19

All of a sudden they heard voices outside. Someone shouted, "Open up!"

Lot went outside and shut the door. He knew the men of that city. He knew that they only wanted to hurt his guests.

"These men are my guests," Lot said. "Please leave them alone."

 Who came to Lot's house?

"Out of our way!" the men shouted. They started to push toward the door.

Just then, the angels opened the door and pulled Lot in. Then they made all the bad men blind.

"You must get out of here!" the angels said. "This city is evil. God is going to destroy it. Quick—get your family and go!"

Lot, his wife, and his two daughters ran for their lives. They got out just in time. Fire came down from the sky and burned up the whole city.

The next morning Sodom was all ashes and black soot. God had destroyed the city because there were no good people left in it.

 Why did God destroy Sodom?

Isaac Is Born

Abram was 99 years old, and Sarai was 89. God had said they would have a family. But they still had no children.

God appeared to Abram. "I am God Almighty. Obey me and follow my ways. If you do, I will make you great. Your new name is Abraham, which means 'father of many.' Sarai shall be called Sarah."

Genesis 17; 21

Abraham laughed. "I am an old man!" he said to himself. "Sarah has never had a child. How can we become 'parents of many'?"

God answered, "I have said it, and it will happen."

Why did Abraham laugh?

"Sarah will have a son," God said. "You will call him Isaac. He will serve me. And I will bless him, just as I have blessed you!"

The next year, Abraham turned 100. Sarah turned 90. And Sarah gave birth to a baby boy!

They named him Isaac, just as God said to do.
Sarah looked at baby Isaac. "What a miracle!" she said. "God has been so good to us!"

 Why was Sarah so happy?

Isaac and Rebekah

Abraham's little baby Isaac grew up. Soon Isaac became a man and wanted to be married.

Abraham said to his servant, "Please help Isaac find a wife. Go to the town of Nahor, and God will guide you to her."

So Abraham's servant set out with ten camels and went to Nahor. There, he stopped by a well.

He prayed, "O Lord, please show me the woman who should be Isaac's wife."

Just then a young woman walked up. She gave him a drink. She gave all his thirsty camels a drink, too.

When she finished, the man said, "May I meet your family?"

Why did Abraham's servant go to Nahor?

"Yes, you may," she answered. She told
Abraham's servant about her family. As soon as she
did, he knew she was the one for Isaac.

Her name was Rebekah.

Abraham's servant met her whole family. "I have
come to help Abraham's son find a wife. I prayed,
and God guided me to Rebekah."

"Do you want to marry Isaac?" her father asked. She said yes!

So Rebekah went back to Canaan with Abraham's servant. And Isaac and Rebekah got married.

 Whom did Rebekah agree to marry?

Jacob and Esau

Isaac was 40 years old when he married Rebekah. But they couldn't have any children.

Isaac and Rebekah were sad. Isaac prayed, "O please, God, let us have a baby!"

Many years later Rebekah gave birth to twin boys. She and Isaac were so happy! They named the boys Esau and Jacob.

Esau became a hunter. He traveled all over the countryside hunting wild animals with a bow and arrows.

But Jacob became a shepherd. He stayed home and cared for sheep and goats.

Their father, Isaac, liked wild meat, so he liked Esau best. Rebekah's favorite was Jacob.

How were Jacob and Esau different?

One day Jacob was home cooking some stew. Esau came home very hungry. "I'm starving," said Esau. "Give me some of that stew!"

But Jacob answered, "Only if you give me your birthright."

A birthright included many special privileges. Only one child in each family had it. Esau had the birthright because he had been born first.

But Esau was so hungry that he didn't care about the birthright

"You can HAVE the birthright!" Esau grumbled. "Just give me that stew!"

Jacob scooped out a bowlful of stew. And Esau gave up his birthright.

 Why did Esau give Jacob his birthright?

Jacob Tricks His Father

Isaac was old and blind. He thought he would soon die.

So Isaac said, "Esau, go out and hunt down a wild animal. Cook it for me just the way I like it. Then I will give you my blessing, and you will become the leader of the family."

Esau wanted his father's blessing more than anything. He jumped up, got his bow and arrows, and went out to hunt.

Rebekah had heard everything. But she wanted Jacob to have the blessing, not Esau. "Jacob," she said quickly, "go get two of our best goats. I will cook them for your father. You can take the food to him and get the blessing yourself."

"But Father will know I am not Esau," said Jacob. "He will curse me, not bless me!"

Who was supposed to get Isaac's blessing?

"Just do as I say," said Rebekah.

So Jacob got two goats, and Rebekah cooked them. Rebekah put goats' hair on Jacob's arms and neck. This made his skin hairy like Esau's.

Then Jacob took the food to his father. He pretended to be Esau. "I have the meal you asked for," Jacob lied.

"So soon?" Isaac asked.

"God helped me," Jacob lied again. Isaac touched Jacob's hairy arms. "Are you really Esau?" he asked. "Yes." Jacob lied once more.

Isaac ate the tasty meal. Then he said, "Now I will give you my blessing."

So Isaac blessed Jacob instead of Esau.

 Why did Jacob get his father's blessing?

Jacob Goes Away

Esau was very angry with his brother. Jacob had tricked him twice. Now Jacob had Esau's birthright AND their father's blessing!

"I am going to kill him!" Esau yelled.

When Rebekah heard this, she got very upset. She didn't want her sons to kill each other.

Genesis 27–28

Rebekah went to Jacob at once. "Your brother wants to kill you," she said. "Go far away to your uncle Laban's house and stay with him until Esau stops being mad. I'll tell you when it's safe to come back home."

So Jacob packed his things and left.

Why did Jacob pack his things?

59

Jacob walked a long way to where Laban lived, far away from Canaan. *What will happen while I am away?* he wondered. Jacob was tired. He found a rock for a pillow and lay down to sleep.

God appeared to him in a dream. Jacob saw angels going up and down a stairway to heaven. God was saying, "I will take care of you, Jacob. Don't worry, you will get to go home someday."

Jacob woke up. Now he knew he would be all right.

He took the rock that was under his head and set it upright to remind him of his dream.

Then he set out again for his uncle Laban's house.

 What did God tell Jacob in his dream?

Jacob Comes Home

Jacob stayed with his uncle Laban for many years.
He worked hard tending sheep and goats.

Year after year God gave him success.
Everything Jacob did went well. He even got married
and had twelve children!

But after 20 years, the time had come for Jacob
to go home. He gathered his family and packed up all
their things.

Genesis 32–33

Jacob sent a messenger ahead of him. "Tell my brother Esau that I am coming," he said.

A little while later, the messenger came back. "Esau is coming to meet you," he said. "And he is bringing 400 men!"

How long was Jacob away from home?

"Oh no!" said Jacob. "He is still mad at me for stealing his birthright and his blessing."

Jacob prayed, "Dear God, you promised to bless me. Save me from my brother, Esau!"

Jacob sent Esau gifts of sheep, goats, cattle, and donkeys. And he kept praying.

The next day came and Jacob looked up. He saw Esau and his 400 men coming toward him! But they didn't attack Jacob. Esau ran to meet his brother. And he hugged him like a best friend.

What did Jacob send to Esau?

Joseph and His Brothers

Jacob loved all of his 12 sons—Gad, Asher, Reuben, Simeon, Levi, Judah, Issachar, Zebulun, Joseph, Benjamin, Dan, and Naphtali—and one daughter, Dinah. But young Joseph was his favorite. Jacob even gave him a fancy coat. Joseph's brothers were so jealous that they started to hate him.

One night Joseph dreamed that he was in charge. He told his brothers all about the dream.

Genesis 37

The next night Joseph dreamed that even his mother and father had to obey him. He told everyone about that dream, too.

"Let's fix that dreamer once and for all," his brothers said. "Let's kill him!"

"No," said Reuben. "Let's just throw him into a pit."

 Why did Joseph's brothers hate him?

They waited until they were out in the fields. Then they grabbed him, took off his fancy coat, and put him into a big pit.

At dinner that evening, they saw some merchants passing through. "Hey," said Judah, "let's sell Joseph to those merchants! At least that way he won't die. He IS our brother, after all."

The brothers all thought that was a good idea. So they sold him to the merchants as a slave.

Before they got home, they made up a big story. The brothers put goat's blood on Joseph's fancy coat to trick their father. "Joseph got killed by a wild animal," they lied.

Jacob was very upset. He just cried and cried.

 Why did Jacob cry?

God Cares for Joseph

The merchants took Joseph to Egypt—a land that was far away from Joseph's home. What would happen to him? Would he ever see his family again?

The merchants sold Joseph to a powerful man named Potiphar. Joseph became Potiphar's slave!

Genesis 39

Joseph had to work hard. But God made him a good worker, and Potiphar noticed.

After a while, Joseph's master put him in charge of the whole house. People had to do whatever Joseph said, just as if Potiphar had said it.

 What did the merchants do with Joseph?

God blessed Potiphar because of Joseph. Things went well for his family.

But one day Potiphar's wife wanted Joseph to do something bad. Joseph said no.

Potiphar's wife got angry. She told lies about Joseph to get him in trouble. Potiphar believed all the lies. Joseph was thrown into jail with the king's prisoners.

Once again, God took care of Joseph. God made him popular with the men in charge of the jail. After a while, they made him keeper of the other prisoners.

And Joseph did a good job because God was with him.

 How did God take care of Joseph in jail?

Joseph Becomes a Ruler

The king of Egypt was mad at his butler and baker. They were sent to the jail where Joseph was.

One night the butler and baker had dreams they did not understand. God showed Joseph what the dreams meant. The butler would get to serve the king again, but the baker would be killed.

"Remember me when you go back to the king," Joseph said to the butler.

The butler got out of jail and returned to serve the king, just as Joseph had said. But the butler forgot about Joseph.

Two years went by. One night the king dreamed that some skinny cows ate some fat cows. He also dreamed that some thin grain ate up some thick grain.

 What did Joseph want the butler to do?

The king wondered, "What do my dreams mean?" But no one could tell him. Then the butler remembered Joseph.

So Joseph was brought from jail. The king told Joseph about his dreams. Joseph said, "For seven years, lots of food will grow. Then for the next seven years, no food will grow."

The king saw that God had made Joseph wise. He put Joseph in charge of all Egypt. Only the king had more authority.

And it all happened just as Joseph said.

 Why was Joseph made ruler?

Joseph Forgives His Brothers

Jacob and his family lived in Canaan. They had no food because no rain had fallen for a long time. So Jacob sent his sons to Egypt to buy food. But Benjamin didn't go because he was the youngest.

The brothers got to Egypt and went to see the ruler. They didn't know that the ruler was Joseph.

But Joseph knew who they were. And he noticed that Benjamin was not with them. "You are spies!" Joseph said.

Genesis 42–45

"No!" they said. "We are shepherds. Our father and youngest brother are waiting for us back home."

"Then go and get your brother, and I'll believe you!" Joseph answered.

So nine of the brothers went home to get Benjamin. Jacob did not want Benjamin to leave, but he had no choice.

 Did Joseph's brothers recognize him?

Joseph really loved his brother Benjamin. He was glad to see him. He invited them all to dinner and gave Benjamin more than anyone else.

Then he said to them, "Benjamin will stay and be my slave." But he was just testing them.

Judah bowed down. "Please let Benjamin go!" he begged. "If he does not return, my father will die of sadness!"

Joseph cried. He could keep his secret no longer.

"I am your brother Joseph!" he said. "I am the one you sold to the merchants. But don't worry—God sent me here to save many lives."

They all hugged and cried. "Now go back and get our father too," Joseph said. "And don't fight along the way!"

So Jacob and their whole family moved to Egypt— 70 people in all. And the king gave them the best land.

 What was Joseph's secret?

Baby Moses

Jacob's family lived in Egypt for many years. After 400 years, his family grew to be thousands and thousands of people. They called themselves Hebrews.

The new king of Egypt didn't like this. "These Hebrews will take over Egypt!" he yelled.

Exodus 1–2

So the king made them slaves. He treated them very badly. They had to work for him and not be paid.

The Hebrews kept having babies. The king didn't like that either.

So he told his people to throw the Hebrew baby boys into the river. The Hebrew mothers were very, very sad.

What was the king afraid of?

One Hebrew woman hid her baby boy. She kept him a secret for three months.

When she could not hide him any longer, she made a boat out of a basket. She put him in it and placed the little boat on the river.

An Egyptian princess found the little boat. "This is one of the Hebrew babies," she said.

The baby's big sister was nearby. "Shall I get a Hebrew woman to feed him for you?" she asked the princess.

"Yes," the princess said. So the girl ran and got her mother. The princess named the baby *Moses*.

So God saved Moses' life. And Moses' mother got to take care of her own baby boy!

 Who found baby Moses?

God Tells Moses to Help

Moses grew up in the king's house. He was a prince. One day, he killed a bad man who was beating a Hebrew slave. He had to leave Egypt. He went to a land far away.

Years and years went by. In Egypt, the Hebrews were still slaves. "Help us, God!" they prayed.

God heard their prayer.

Exodus 2–4

One day Moses saw a burning bush. He thought, *The bush burns and burns, but it doesn't turn into ashes.*

Then Moses heard God speak. "My people are hurting," God said. "I want to help them!" Moses shook with fear and covered his face.

Why was Moses afraid?

"I want you to lead my people out of Egypt,"
God said. "You will take them to a good and
wonderful land."

"Me?" Moses asked.

"Yes. I will be with you," God answered.

"But what if the leaders don't listen to me?"
Moses asked.

God made a stick turn into a snake. Then God
said, "Miracles like this will make them listen."

"But I can't talk very well," Moses said.

"I made your mouth!" God said. "I will tell you what to say."

Moses still didn't want to go. But God promised that Aaron, Moses' brother, would help. So Moses left for Egypt.

 How would God help Moses?

89

The King Says No

Moses and Aaron went to the king of Egypt. "You have made God's people your slaves," they said. "God wants you to let them go!"

But the king answered, "Who is God? Why should I listen to him? I am the KING. The answer is no!"

God said to Moses, "I will show that king who's in charge. Then he will let my people go." So God made ten terrible things happen in Egypt.

Exodus 5–10

God turned the Nile River into blood. The Egyptians could not drink the water anymore. The king said, "OK, you can go." But when God made the river into water again, the king changed his mind.

So God sent bunches and bunches of frogs. At first the king said, "OK, you can go." But the frogs went away, and the king changed his mind again.

 What did Moses want the king to do?

Then clouds of gnats and flies came. Egypt's farm animals died. The Egyptians got sick. Hailstones knocked down many of their crops. Then grasshoppers ate the rest. It got dark as night for three days.

Sometimes the king would say, "OK, you can go" or "Some of you can go." But each time the king would change his mind.

And each time the king got madder and madder.
After the three days of darkness, he said to Moses,
"My final answer is no. Do not ask me again!"

Moses said, "OK. I will not ask you again!"

 What happened to Egypt's farm animals?

God's People Are Free!

The king of Egypt was very stubborn. God told him nine times to free the slaves. But each time the king said no.

So God sent Moses to the king one more time. "God has a message for you, King. Tonight the oldest son in every family in Egypt will die. Even your own son will die! Then you will BEG God's people to leave."

The king got mad, and Moses left.

Exodus 11–12

Moses said to the Hebrews, "Cook a special meal. Have some lamb and some flat bread. And be ready to leave in the middle of your meal.

"Also, mark your door with some of the lamb's blood. This will show that you are God's people, and your sons will be safe."

What had God told the king to do?

Then God said, "That day will be a new holiday for you. It will be called Passover, since I will pass over your houses when I punish the king."

God's people did what God said, but the Egyptians didn't. And that night, the oldest son in every Egyptian family died. Even the king's oldest son died. But all the children of God's people were safe.

Finally, the king said to Moses, "Take your people and go!"

So Moses, Aaron, and all God's people left Egypt. That is how God rescued them from being slaves in Egypt.

What new holiday did the Hebrews celebrate?

Through the Sea

God's people left Egypt just as God said. They marched out together—over 2 million people!

God showed them where to go. He led them with a big, tall cloud. At night a big, tall fire led the way. How happy they were!

All of a sudden they saw an army coming. It was the Egyptians.

Exodus 14–15

God's people were in the desert by the seashore. They had nowhere to go. They were trapped!

God's people shook with fear. "It would have been better to stay in Egypt," they said to Moses. "Now we're going to die!"

Why were God's people afraid?

But Moses said, "Don't be afraid. God will fight for you!"

Just then, God made a strong wind blow. It made the sea split in two. God's people walked into the sea, right down the middle, on dry ground.

The Egyptians followed them into the sea. But God made their chariot wheels fall off.

"God is helping his people!" they said. "Let's get out of here!"

But it was too late. The walls of water fell down again. The whole army was covered.

God's people were already on the other side. They were safe!

How did God help his people?

Miriam's Song

Moses led God's people out of Egypt. The Egyptians tried to stop them, but God did a mighty miracle. He made an escape route for them through the sea.

Now God's people could go to a new and better land—a land of their very own!

So they sang a song.

> "Sing to the Lord,
> for he is very great!

Exodus 15

He stopped the chariots,
and he saved us from the warriors.

"The Egyptians bragged.
They said they would get us.
But YOU got THEM, Lord.
You made the sea cover them up.

 Why did God's people sing?

"You have been very good to us, Lord!
Hooray! Thank you, God!"

Miriam was Moses' sister. She played a
tambourine as she sang. And she led the women in
dancing and singing.

Again and again they sang:

"Sing to the Lord,
for he is very great!
He stopped the chariots,
and he saved us from the warriors!

"Hooray! Thank you, God!"

 What instrument did Miriam play?

God Sends Food

God's people had been walking in the desert. They had no food. They were very hungry.

They went to Moses and Aaron. "You should have let us die in Egypt," they said. "At least we weren't hungry there. We could eat all we wanted. But out here, we are starving!"

God spoke to Moses. "I will make food fall from heaven, right onto the ground. Tell the people to get as much as they need each morning. On Friday, gather enough for Saturday too. Then you can rest from having to get food one day a week."

Moses and Aaron told this to the people.

What did the people complain about?

The next morning, there was a layer of white stuff on the ground. The people got up and said, "What is it?"

Moses said, "It is the bread God told you about. Take just enough for each person in your family. Don't take any extra."

So the people gathered all they needed, and everyone had enough. Each morning they would get up, and there would be the food. They would gather it and eat it. It tasted like wafers of honey.

They called it manna, which means, "What is it?"

 How did God feed his people?

The Ten Commandments

God led his people to a mountain called Mt. Sinai. Moses climbed up the mountain, and God spoke to him there.

"I brought you out of Egypt. Obey me so that all will go well with you."

Moses gave God's message to the people. And God's people said, "We will do whatever God says."

Then God gave Moses ten rules for the people to obey:

"Don't worship any other gods.
"Don't make little gods out of rocks or metal.
"Don't say 'God' unless you're talking to me.
"Work for six days, then rest one day.

What did God tell Moses?

"Obey your father and mother.
"Don't kill people.
"Don't love another man's wife.
"Don't steal.
"Don't lie.
"Don't want what other people have."

God wrote all these rules on two pieces of stone. They were called the Ten Commandments. Moses told these rules to God's people.

And the people promised to obey them all.

 What did God's people promise to obey?

Aaron's Bad Mistake

Moses went up the mountain to talk to God. He was up there a long time. God's people got tired of waiting for him.

So they said to Aaron, Moses' brother, "Make a god for us. We are tired of waiting for Moses."

"OK," said Aaron. "Give me your gold earrings."

Exodus 32

Aaron melted down the gold. He took some tools and shaped the gold into a cow. When he was all done, he said, "This is your god!"

All the people cheered. "This is the god that saved us from Egypt!" they said.

Aaron made a place for them to worship the cow. "We'll have a party tomorrow," he said.

What did Aaron do with the people's gold?

Up on the mountain, God said to Moses. "The people are sinning. They have made a god out of gold. Go down the mountain, quickly!"

Moses ran down. He had the Ten Commandments with him. When he saw the people singing to the cow, he got angry. He threw the tablets on the ground. "Why have you let the people do this?" he asked Aaron.

Aaron lied. "I didn't do anything bad. They gave me their gold, and I threw it in the fire. Then this cow just came out!"

But God knew the truth. He punished the people because they said the cow was a god.

 What lie did Aaron tell?

God's People Get Scared

God's people came to the land God wanted to give them. Moses chose 12 men. He told them, "Find out what kind of land it is. What are the people like?"

The men went into the land for 40 days. Then they came back. "The land is great!" they said. "It has lots of good food."

Numbers 13–14

Then they said, "But the people are very big and strong. They will not let us have the land."

Two of the men, named Caleb and Joshua, said, "We should go into the land. God will help us!"

 What kind of land did the 12 men find?

But the other 10 men said, "Those big, strong people will squash us like grasshoppers!"

God's people cried. They were scared of the big people. They did not think God could give them the land.

But Joshua and Caleb said, "The land is good, and God is with us. Let's go!"

"No!" said the people "Let's kill Moses and get a new leader!"

Just then God stopped them. "You are stubborn!" he said. "Since you won't do what I say, you will walk around in the desert for 40 years. I will give the land to your children."

And that's just what happened.

 Why did God's people want to kill Moses?

A Donkey Talks

God's people came to a land called Moab. The king of Moab, named Balak, wanted God's people to go away.

So King Balak sent for a man named Balaam. Balaam did magic.

King Balak sent messengers to Balaam. "Come and curse God's people so they will leave," they said. "If you do, King Balak will make you rich and famous."

Numbers 22

Balaam answered, "I can't curse God's people. But I will go to Moab." Balaam wanted to be rich and famous. He got on his donkey and headed for Moab.

While Balaam was riding along, an angel appeared in the road to stop him. But Balaam didn't see the angel and kept going.

 What did Balak want Balaam to do?

Balaam's donkey saw the angel and stopped. Balaam hit the donkey and shouted, "Get going, you lazy donkey!"

The donkey asked, "Why are you beating me?"

Balaam answered, "Because you are making me look dumb!" Just then Balaam saw the angel.

"Your donkey is a lot smarter than you are!" the angel said.

Balaam was afraid. "I have sinned!" he said. "Do you want me to go back home?"

"No, go to Moab. But do not curse God's people—bless them!"

So Balaam went to Moab and blessed God's people. He finally acted as smart as his donkey!

 What did the donkey see?

Rahab Helps God's People

After Moses died, Joshua became the leader of God's people. It was time for them to enter Canaan, the land that God had promised them.

Joshua sent two spies to check out the city of Jericho. They found a place to spend the night.

But the Jericho police found out that the spies were there. Officers came pounding on the door.

126

Joshua 2

"We've come to arrest those spies!" they yelled.

Rahab, the owner of the house, answered, "Those men already left. I didn't know they were spies. If you hurry you might catch them!"

The police went looking for the spies outside the city.

 Why did the spies go to Jericho?

But the spies had not left Rahab's house. They were up on the roof, hiding.

Rahab went up to talk to them. "I know who you are," she whispered. "Everyone in the city is afraid of you. We have all heard about how great your God is. If I help you, will you help me and my family?"

"Yes," the men said.

So Rahab helped them escape. She let the spies out through a window. They climbed down a rope and got out of Jericho safely!

 How did Rahab help the spies?

Walls Fall Down

The city of Jericho was like a big fort. It had huge stone walls around it. It had a big gate in front that was locked. No one could get in or out.

God's people, the people of Israel, were outside. God told Joshua, "Don't attack the city. Instead, tell your army to walk around it once each day. The priests will follow, each carrying a trumpet.

Joshua 6

"Then on the seventh day, tell the priests to blow their trumpets as they go. Tell them to march around the city seven times. The seventh time around, tell everyone to give a mighty shout. Then the city walls will fall down!"

Joshua told his men what God had said. They got ready to march.

 What was Jericho like?

The people of Israel marched around the city once a day for six days.

On the seventh day they marched around seven times. The priests blew their trumpets as they marched.

The seventh time around, all the people gave a mighty shout. The walls of Jericho shook and crumbled and fell down flat!

The people of Israel captured the city.

But they didn't forget Rahab. They rescued her and her family, just as they had promised. And Rahab's family got to live with God's people.

 What happened when the people shouted?

Gideon

The people of Israel lived happily in their new land of Canaan. God had given it to them.

But other groups of people lived in the land, too. One group was the people of Midian. They were cruel and mean. They stole food and animals from the people of Israel. This happened so much that the people of Israel had nothing left. They were not happy anymore.

So they prayed for help.

Judges 6–7

Then God spoke to a man named Gideon. "Gather an army, Gideon!" God said.

Gideon found 32,000 men willing to fight.

But God said, "That's too many. If you win, you'll think you did it without my help. Make your army smaller!"

So Gideon sent home all the men who were afraid. Only 10,000 remained.

What did God want Gideon to do?

"That's still too many," God said. So Gideon sent 9,700 more home. Only 300 remained.

Gideon and his 300 men waited for night. They sneaked up to the army of Midian and stood in the darkness around the camp. Each one had a clay jar with a torch inside.

Gideon's orders were: "Wait for my signal. When I shout, break your jars and give a loud shout."

Gideon gave the signal. All his men broke their jars and shouted. The soldiers of Midian woke up. They ran around in confusion and began fighting each other. Gideon and his men chased them all away.

Now the land was safe. God had helped Gideon win, just as he had promised!

 How did Gideon win?

Mighty Samson

Before Samson was born, God chose him to do a special job. God told his parents, "Samson will become a great hero. But he must never cut his hair."

The people of Israel had cruel enemies called Philistines. Samson's special job was to defeat them.

As Samson grew up, God gave him great strength. The Philistines could not even scare him.

They tried many times to catch Samson. But each time, he would escape. And if they tried to fight him, Samson always won, even when there were 1,000 men against him.

Then Samson met a woman named Delilah. "Tell me the secret of your strength," she asked sweetly. At first Samson said no.

What was Samson's special job?

But after many times he said, "OK, I'll tell you. If you cut my hair, I'll be weak."

The next time Samson fell asleep, Delilah let some Philistines sneak in. They cut off his hair and tied him up. When Samson woke up, he could not get away. He was not strong anymore.

The Philistines had a big party. "Samson is our prisoner!" they sang.

But Samson was sorry he had broken his promise to God. He prayed, "God, let me be strong one more time!"

So God made Samson strong again. Samson pushed on the pillars nearby with all his might. "Argh!" They fell, and the whole building fell with them. He and all his enemies died.

 How did Samson lose his strength?

Kind Ruth

Naomi was old and lived far from her home. Her husband had died. Her two sons had died. And she had no children or grandchildren.

One of Naomi's sons had married a woman named Ruth. Ruth was very kind to Naomi. But Naomi wanted to go back home to the land of Israel. Ruth wasn't from the land of Israel.

Naomi was very sad. She thought she would be all alone.

Ruth 1–4

But Ruth said, "Let me go with you. Your people will be my people. Your God will be my God!"

So Ruth went with Naomi to Bethlehem. But Naomi was still sad. "I have no children to take care of me," she said sadly.

Ruth went out into a field to pick up leftover grain for food.

 Why was Naomi sad?

The field was owned by a man named Boaz, one of Naomi's relatives.

Boaz heard how kind Ruth had been to Naomi. He noticed how hard Ruth worked.

Boaz liked Ruth. He told his workers to leave extra grain for her. Every day, Ruth came home with plenty of food for herself and Naomi.

Naomi was pleased. "God is taking care of us after all," she said.

Soon Ruth and Boaz got married. And it wasn't long before Ruth had a son. They named him Obed.

Naomi was so happy—now she even had a grandson!

Why was Naomi happy?

Young Samuel

Hannah cried and cried. "What's the matter?" her husband, Elkanah, asked.

"I wish we could have a child," she said. For Hannah had never had a baby.

"Dear God," Hannah prayed, "if you will give me a child, I will let him serve you."

The next year God did a miracle—Hannah had a baby boy! She named him Samuel.

1 Samuel 1–3

Hannah was so happy that she praised God with a song:

"I am so glad, Lord!
You are very good to me!"

Hannah did not forget her promise to God. So she brought Samuel to the temple. There he would grow up and learn to serve God as a priest.

 What made Hannah glad?

So the boy Samuel stayed with Eli the priest. Each year Hannah would make him a new coat. Samuel kept growing, and everybody liked him.

Then one night Samuel heard a voice call his name. Samuel went to Eli. "Here I am, sir. What do you want?"

"I did not call you," said Eli.

Samuel went back to bed, but he heard the voice again.

So Eli said, "Go back to bed. When you hear the voice again, say, 'Yes, Lord. I am listening.' "

Samuel did as Eli said. And God gave him a message that night. From that day on Samuel was a prophet—a special messenger for God. He became the leader of all Israel!

Who was calling to Samuel?

Israel's First King

The people of Israel had no king. But they wanted one because all the other nations had one.

Their leader, Samuel, said it was a bad idea. "God is your king. A human king will just tax you and make you work harder."

But the leaders would not listen. "Give us a king anyway!" they said again.

1 Samuel 8–11

Samuel asked God what to do.

"Go ahead and give them a king," God answered. "A man named Saul will soon come to you for help. Make him the king."

Samuel went home and waited for Saul to arrive. Just as God had said, Saul came to see him.

What did the people of Israel want?

151

"Come with me," Samuel said. "I have a special message from God for you." They walked to the edge of the town.

Then Samuel took a flask of olive oil, poured it on Saul's head, and said, "You are now the king!" And the Spirit of God came upon Saul.

Later, all the leaders of Israel and all the people said, "Long live King Saul!"

At first Saul was afraid to lead the people. Some people didn't think he should be king.

But when an enemy army attacked a city of Israel, Saul got mad. He gathered an army and fought back. Saul's army won.

Then everyone cheered. They were glad Saul was their king.

 What was Saul's first job as king?

David

Saul was the king of Israel. But he did not obey God. He did whatever he wanted, even if it was wrong.

So Samuel told Saul, "God wants Israel's king to obey him. He has chosen another man to replace you."

God told Samuel to go to Bethlehem. "The new king I have chosen lives there," God said. "I will show you who he is."

When Samuel got to Bethlehem, God led him to a man named Jesse, who had eight sons. Samuel took one look at the oldest and thought, *He must be the new king!*

But God said, "You are thinking only of what he looks like. I don't care about that. I care about the kind of person he is. This is not the one."

 Why did God want a different king?

Jesse had six other sons with him. Samuel asked God about them, one by one. But each time, God said, "He is not the one."

Finally Samuel asked Jesse, "Are these all your sons?"

"The youngest is taking care of sheep," Jesse answered.

"Go get him," said Samuel.

So Jesse brought in his youngest son, David. Right then God said, "He's the one!"

So Samuel named David the next king. Then David knew that he would be king after Saul.

Why did Samuel choose David?

David and Goliath

Goliath and David stood across from each other. Goliath was tall and big and sweaty—bigger and taller and meaner than every Israelite there. He looked fierce and angry. He wore a bronze helmet and heavy armor. He carried a spear, javelin, and sword.

"Am I a dog," Goliath roared, "that you attack me with a stick?"

158

1 Samuel 17

David looked right at Goliath and said, "You come against me with sword and spear and javelin. But I come against you in the name of the Lord Almighty. God doesn't need a sword or a spear. This battle is the Lord's, and he will give you into my hands."

As Goliath moved in to attack, David ran straight at him.

 Who did David depend on to help him?

159

Reaching into his bag, David pulled out a stone. He put the stone in his sling, swung it around, and let it fly.

The rock sailed through the air and struck Goliath right in the forehead. The giant warrior cried out, "Arrgh!" He dropped his spear and fell to the ground in a heap.

David ran to Goliath, took out the giant's sword, and killed him.

The Philistine army ran for their lives. All the Israelites cheered! David was a hero.

 What did David use to fight Goliath?

Saul Is Jealous

David became a hero after he killed Goliath. King Saul brought him to the palace. "Stay here and work for me—I insist!"

So David became Saul's personal helper. David played his harp for Saul whenever Saul felt sad. Saul even put him in charge of his troops.

Prince Jonathan liked David, too. In fact, they became best friends.

So David lived in the palace as a favorite guest.
Everyone else liked David, too. The people even made up a song that went:

"Saul can beat 1,000 enemies,
But David can beat 10,000 enemies!"

What was David's new job?

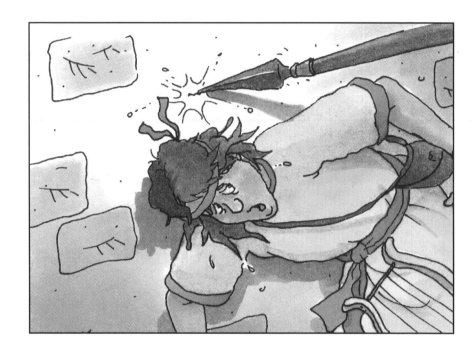

When Saul heard the people singing about how great David was, he became VERY angry. "Why do they say David can beat more men than I can?" he fumed. He could hardly stand it.

The next day Saul was still upset. David played music as usual to calm him down. But all of a sudden, Saul jumped up and threw a spear at David. David jumped to the side, and the spear stuck in the wall!

David dropped his harp and ran for his life.

From then on, Saul wanted to kill him. So David had to run away and hide from Saul.

But God was with David. Many men joined his small army. The people liked him even more than before.

What did Saul try to do to David?

David Shows Mercy

David had 600 loyal men. They stayed with him and obeyed his orders. They went wherever he went.

But David had to keep running. Saul was trying to kill him.

Prince Jonathan was on David's side. "Don't worry," he said, "Saul won't catch you. I will always be your friend. And you will be the next king."

1 Samuel 23–24

David and his men fled to a place called Engedi. It was a rocky area full of caves. David and his men hid in the caves.

Saul found out where they were. He got 3,000 of his best soldiers and went to Engedi. When they got there, Saul went into one of the caves alone.

 Where did David hide?

David and his men were in that very cave. They whispered to him, "God said you would be king, David. Now's your chance to kill Saul!"

David showed mercy. He sneaked up and only cut off a corner of Saul's robe.

Saul left the cave. He could not find David or his men. When he got ready to leave, David followed him.

"Saul!" David yelled. "I had the chance to kill you. See this piece of your robe? I'm not trying to harm YOU. Why are you trying to kill ME?"

Saul cried. "You are a better man than I, David," he said. "Now I know you will become king. Promise you will not kill me when you do!"

David promised, and Saul went home.

 What did David do for Saul?

A New King

God wanted David to be the king after Saul. After Saul died, some leaders of Israel crowned David king.

But some men didn't want David to be king. They crowned their own king–Saul's son. They fought against David.

But God was with David, and David won.

2 Samuel 2–5

Leaders from all over Israel then came to David. They promised to be loyal to him. They said, "The Lord has made you king. Long live King David!"

David then led his army to Jerusalem. That's where David wanted his capital to be. David attacked the city and captured it.

Who was the new king of Israel?

People called it the City of David. David made it bigger. He also put new walls around it.

David had a good friend—King Hiram of Tyre. Hiram helped David build a palace.

David praised and thanked God for this. "You are kind to us, God!" David sang.

But some enemies called Philistines tried to stop David. David asked God what to do. "Fight them. You will win!" God said. So David fought them and won.

"You did it, God!" David said. "You beat our enemies!"

Then, at last, there was peace.

 Who helped David?

Wise King Solomon

David grew to be an old man. Soon it was too hard for him to be king. "Nathan! Zadok!" he called to his trusted helpers. "It is time to make my son Solomon king."

They did so. And David said to his son, "Obey God, Solomon. If you do, God will bless you."

So Solomon became king after David.

1 Kings 1–3

God appeared to Solomon in a dream. "Ask for anything you like," God said.

Solomon answered, "I feel as helpless as a little boy. I'm not ready to rule this nation. Please give me wisdom so I'll be a good king."

God was very pleased with Solomon. "Because you did not ask for long life or lots of money or great power, I will make you the wisest person on earth. I will also make you rich and famous."

 What did Solomon ask for?

Soon after, two women came to Solomon. They were fighting over a little baby. "He's my baby!" one woman said.

"No he isn't," said the other. "Yours died by accident and you took mine!"

But God had made Solomon very wise. And because Solomon was wise, he knew that the real mother wanted to protect her baby more than anything else.

So he said, "Cut the baby in two! And give each woman half!"

"No!" the real mother yelled. "Let the other woman have the baby!"

176

Now Solomon knew who the real mother was. He let her have her baby back.

Everyone heard about it. "Wow," people said. "Solomon is really wise!" The news even spread to other countries. And people came from all over to hear his wisdom.

 What argument did Solomon settle?

God's Great Temple

The people of Israel served God. But they had no temple or church.

King David had wanted to build a temple. But God said, "Let Solomon do it." So when Solomon became king, he got started right away.

Solomon told everyone to pitch in. Stonecutters, wood-carvers, and other workers came from all over Israel.

1 Kings 5–8

Even King Hiram of Tyre, the country to the
north, helped out. He sent lumber.

The stonecutters cut big, huge blocks of stone out
of the ground. They used these for the walls.

The wood-carvers made boards of cedar. They
made panels for all the walls and ceilings inside.

 Who started building the temple?

179

The outside was decorated with gold, silver, and carved wood. The wood-carvers made fancy designs of flowers.

After seven years of work, they finished. "Praise God!" Solomon said.

And he prayed, "You are too great for this little temple, God. But please be with us when we worship. Hear us when we pray. We praise you!"

Then the king and all his people worshiped God in their new temple for the first time. It was amazing—a truly holy place. God's presence stayed with them there. They worshiped and celebrated for two weeks!

 Why did God's people celebrate?

Bold Elijah

The people of Israel did not always follow God. Sometimes they followed pretend gods that they had made up.

King Ahab worshiped a made-up god called Baal. He led many of the people to worship Baal.

That's why God sent the prophet Elijah. "You have led God's people the wrong way," he told Ahab. "You must obey God, not Baal!"

1 Kings 18

But Ahab wouldn't listen. He built worship places for Baal all over Israel.

Finally, God told Elijah to go to Ahab. "Let's see whose god is real," Elijah said to Ahab. "You call on Baal to send fire to light the wood on your altar, and I'll call on God. The god who answers is the true God!"

"OK!" Ahab agreed.

 What did Ahab worship?

Ahab's prophets of Baal went first. They prayed
for hours, "Send fire, Baal!" They even cut themselves
with knives. But nothing happened.

Elijah made fun of them. "Maybe he is sleeping.
Yell louder!"

So they screamed louder. Still nothing
happened. Finally, they gave up.

Then Elijah prayed, "O God, please show everyone that you are real!"

Instantly fire came down from heaven. It burned up everything on Elijah's altar. Everyone cried out, "The Lord is God! The Lord is God!"

 Whom did Elijah worship?

The Boy Who Became King

An evil woman named Athaliah became queen of
Israel. She did this by trying to kill all the princes in
the royal family.

Only one-year-old Joash escaped. His aunt and
uncle snatched him away just in time. They hid him
in the temple.

Athaliah did not know that Joash was alive. She
thought all her enemies were dead.

2 Chronicles 22–23

While Athaliah ruled, Joash's aunt and uncle raised the little prince in secret. It was very lonely. Joash could never go out to play because no one could know about him.

But when Joash turned seven, his uncle got up his courage. He told some friends about Joash.

 Why couldn't Joash go out to play?

"God said that David's family should rule," he said. "It's time to crown Joash king!"

So they made a plan. Other leaders helped them. When the time was right, they brought Joash out of hiding. They had a small army of soldiers around him in the middle of the temple. They put a crown on his head and yelled, "Long live King Joash!"

Athaliah heard them and tried to stop them. But the guards took her away.

So young Joash became king. God saved the people of Israel. Once again, everyone could live in peace.

 Who didn't want Joash to be king?

Jonah and the Big Fish

God sent many prophets to his people. These prophets were special messengers. God told them what to say to the people.

If people were doing bad things, the prophets would say, "You must stop what you're doing and obey God's laws."

If people were doing good things, the prophets would say, "You are doing well. God will reward you!"

Jonah was a prophet. God wanted him to speak to the bad people of Nineveh. But Jonah hated those people because they were mean and evil. He did not want to tell them about God. So he got on a ship and sailed far away.

Who tried to run away from God?

191

God caused a fierce storm at sea. The wind and waves crashed against the ship. Jonah knew that God wanted him to go back. So he said to the crew, "You must throw me overboard to stop the storm!"

The sailors threw Jonah into the sea. The storm stopped. And Jonah prayed, "Save me, God! I'm going to drown!" God made a big fish swallow Jonah. He was in the belly of the fish three days. Jonah prayed and prayed.

Then the fish swam near the shore and spit Jonah out. Jonah thanked God.

"Go to Nineveh, Jonah!" God said. This time Jonah obeyed. The people of Nineveh listened. They stopped doing evil and obeyed God's laws. "I will not destroy the city after all," God said.

 How did Jonah get to the shore?

Hezekiah Prays

King Hezekiah was afraid. His city, Jerusalem, was going to be attacked. The huge enemy army had already destroyed many other cities.

"Why don't you just give up?" the enemy leader yelled. "You can't stop us. We're too strong. God won't help you, either. He sent us to destroy you!"

Isaiah 36–37

Hezekiah knew that his small army could never stop the enemy without God's help.

Hezekiah sent messengers to the prophet Isaiah.

"Pray for us," the message said. "Maybe God will save us." Then Hezekiah went to the temple and prayed.

 Who prayed?

"O God," Hezekiah prayed, "only you can stop this mighty army. You heard them make fun of us. Please save us!"

The prophet Isaiah delivered a message from God. "Don't worry, Hezekiah," the message said. "This big, mean army will lose. They have made fun of me, too, and I will punish them."

That night the enemy army was destroyed by an angel. Hezekiah's army did not even have to fight! The enemy king who ordered the attack was killed, too. God rescued his people!

 Who delivered God's message to Hezekiah?

Lonely Jeremiah

Jeremiah was a prophet. He lived when God's people were not obeying God. They were doing bad things all the time.

"Stop doing evil!" Jeremiah warned. "If you don't, an army will come and defeat you. They will take you far away. And you will have to live there for 70 years before you are allowed to return."

Jeremiah 37; 39

Jeremiah didn't want to bring bad news. But he had to tell the people God's message.

No one listened. They said, "Whose side are you on? You talk like one of our enemies. Now be quiet. Everything will be fine." They put Jeremiah in prison, and then they tried to kill him.

 Why didn't God's people like Jeremiah?

Then one day the army of Babylon attacked
Jerusalem. The army broke through the walls and took
over the city.

The Babylonians captured Zedekiah, king of
Israel. They set fire to the temple and tore down its
walls. They took all the gold and silver they could find.
And they tore down the walls that protected the city.

Then the army took many of God's people away
to Babylon. God's people had to leave their homes.
They had to leave behind all they owned.

Jeremiah was very sad. Everything had happened
just as God had said.

 Where did God's people have to go?

Ezekiel and the Bones

Ezekiel lived in Babylon with God's people. They were very sad. They wanted to go home. They were sorry they had disobeyed God. They sang sad songs about going home.

"O Jerusalem," they sang. "We miss you so much! May we never forget about you!"

Ezekiel 37

One day God took Ezekiel to a valley. It was full of dry bones.

"Speak to the bones, Ezekiel!" God said.

Ezekiel said, "Be alive again!" The bones came together as Ezekiel watched. *Clatter, clatter,* he heard.

What did Ezekiel see?

The skeletons became live people again. All the people were healthy and strong!

"Tell my people about this," God said.

So Ezekiel said to God's people, "Don't be sad. You are here because you did bad things. You were stubborn and would not listen to God. But you are like these bones. One day God will let you go home. God will make you come alive, just as he made the bones come alive."

The people were glad when they heard this. They knew that God still loved them. "I will not leave you here forever," God said. "I will bring you back to the land of Israel. One day, I will let you go back to your homes."

 What did God promise his people?

The Very Hot Furnace

The king of Babylon wanted everyone to know that HE was in charge. So he had a huge gold statue made. Everyone had to bow down and worship it. But three young Jewish men would not bow down.

"WHAT?" the king yelled. "Bring them to me!" The three men were brought to the king. "Is it true that you will not bow down to my statue?"

Daniel 3

"Yes," they answered.

"If you will not bow down, you will be thrown into a very hot furnace!"

But the three men said, "God can protect us from your very hot furnace. But even if he does not, we will not bow down to your statue!"

The king yelled, "Throw them into the furnace!"

 What did the king want everyone to do?

The guards tied up the three men and threw them into the furnace. It was so hot that some of the guards were killed by the heat!

But the king saw an amazing thing in the fire. "I see FOUR men in there. They aren't tied up. And one looks like a god!" God had sent an angel to protect the three men.

"Men of God, come out of there!" the king said. The three men were named Shadrach, Meshach, and Abednego. They came out. They were not hurt, and they did not even smell like smoke!

The king was so amazed that he praised God.

 Who protected the three men?

The Writing on the Wall

The king of Babylon was having a great feast. The guests drank from cups stolen out of God's temple. "We praise you, gods of gold and silver!" they said to their idols.

All of a sudden a big hand appeared in the air. Everyone watched as the hand wrote on the wall. It wrote words in their language. But they did not know what the words meant.

Daniel 5

The king shook with fear. "Bring the fortune-tellers!" he ordered.

The fortune-tellers came. But they did not know what the writing meant.

Someone said, "Daniel can tell you what it means." Daniel was a prophet.

 What scared the king?

The king had Daniel brought in. "Tell me what the writing means!" the king said.

"The writing is a message from God," answered Daniel. "Here is what it means: There is only one God, O King. He is the living God of heaven. Yet you praise gods of gold and silver. The writing says that you will not live much longer. God is looking for rulers who will obey him.

"You will soon die. And your kingdom will be split in two."

That night the city came under attack. The attackers killed the king and split the kingdom in two. It happened just as Daniel had said.

 What happened to the king?

Daniel in the Lions' Den

Daniel was a leader. He was the best leader of all. The king liked him very much. But the other leaders were jealous of him. "Let's get Daniel in trouble," they said.

They knew that Daniel prayed to God. So they said to the king, "We think you should make a new law. Anyone who prays to any god or man, except to you, O King, will be thrown into the den of lions."

Daniel 6

"That sounds good," said the king. So he made it a law.

The jealous leaders sneaked around watching Daniel. Daniel prayed three times a day, so they soon caught him praying to God.

They brought this news to the king.

 What did Daniel do every day?

The king was very upset. He didn't want Daniel to die. But there was nothing he could do. The law was the law.

So Daniel was thrown to the mean and hungry lions. "May God keep you safe, Daniel!" the king said. That night the king couldn't eat or sleep. He wondered if Daniel would be safe.

But God protected Daniel. The next morning, the king went to the den of lions. "Daniel!" the king shouted. "Did God keep you safe?"

"Oh yes!" Daniel replied. "God knows I haven't done anything wrong."

The king was very happy and set Daniel free. The jealous leaders were thrown to the fierce lions instead.

 Why didn't the lions eat Daniel?

Brave Queen Esther

Haman was a powerful friend of the king. Everyone had to bow down to him. But there was a man named Mordecai who would not bow down.

Haman was very angry. *Mordecai is a Jew,* he thought. *I'll show him!*

So Haman made plans to have ALL the Jews killed. He set a date for it and told the whole kingdom.

Mordecai was Queen Esther's cousin. Mordecai sent her a message that said: "Please ask the king to stop Haman!"

Esther 1–10

But Esther said, "I can't go to the king unless he calls for me. If I do, he may have me killed!"

Mordecai said, "You're Jewish, too. Maybe you were made queen so you could help God's people."

"Then pray for me," Esther said. "I will go to the king. And if I die, I die."

Esther went to see the king. But he was not angry when she came. He was glad. "Ask anything you wish," he told her.

What did Mordecai want Esther to do?

"Please, Your Majesty," she said, "I want you and Haman to be my guests at dinner."

The king was delighted. He and Haman went to dinner with Esther that evening. Haman felt honored.

The next evening they had dinner with Esther again. "What is your request, my queen?" the king said. "I will give you up to half my empire!"

"I fear for my life," Queen Esther answered. "Please protect me from harm!"

The king got so angry he stood up. "Who would dare harm you?"

"Haman!" Esther said.

The king then learned about Haman's evil plot to kill the Jews. Haman was arrested and put to death. And the king allowed Mordecai to make a law to protect Esther and all the Jews!

 How did Esther help God's people?

A New Temple

God's people were forced to live in a country called Babylon for 70 years. But God did not forget them.

"You may go back to Israel!" the king of Babylon said. "You are free."

God's people were very excited! They packed their things and got ready to leave. Their neighbors and even the king gave them gifts. They could hardly wait to get back to Jerusalem.

When they arrived, the temple was a wreck. They started fixing it right away.

They bought logs from up north. They cut blocks of stone from out of the ground. Everyone pitched in.

Some enemies tried to stop them. They lied to the king and said, "These people are troublemakers."

Where had God's people been living?

At first the workers had to stop. "Now we'll never finish the temple," they said sadly.

But then God sent prophets who said, "Don't stop building! God is with you!" The workers felt brave again and went back to work. The king said it was OK.

After many years of hard work, they finished.

"Hurray!" they shouted. Finally God's temple was rebuilt. Finally they could worship God as they had before.

They had a big party. They worshiped God and praised him. They remembered the time when God rescued their people from Egypt many years before. It was a joyous, happy time in Israel once again.

 What did God's people rebuild?

A Wall for God's City

Nehemiah loved God. He worked for the king in Babylon. He often wondered how God's people in Israel were doing.

One day Nehemiah got some bad news. "The people in Israel are not doing well. The temple has been rebuilt, but the walls of Jerusalem are still broken down. God's enemies are laughing!"

Nehemiah was very upset. He prayed, "Dear God, please let me help them!"

Nehemiah 1–13

Nehemiah was so upset that it showed on his face. The king noticed and said, "What is the matter, Nehemiah?"

"My people need help," Nehemiah answered. "Please let me go and help them."

The king said yes. Nehemiah left right away.

Why was Nehemiah upset?

When Nehemiah got to Jerusalem, he said to the leaders, "Our city is in ruins. Let's rebuild the walls and make it strong again!" They agreed, and soon the work began.

It was hard and dangerous. They had only a few workers. Enemies came and said, "Stop building right now!"

But Nehemiah prayed, "Protect us, Lord!" And he said to the workers, "Don't be afraid! God will help us!"

Half of the men worked while half stood guard. Their enemies didn't attack. And after only 52 days, the city had big, strong walls around it. The gates had big, strong doors. God's city was safe!

The people celebrated. They confessed their sins and promised to obey God. And they sang, "Praise the Lord!"

 How long did it take to rebuild the city walls?

John the Baptist Is Born

One day the priest Zechariah was working in the temple. The angel Gabriel appeared to him. "Your wife is going to have a son," Gabriel said. "He will be a great prophet. You will name him John."

Zechariah was surprised. He and his wife, Elizabeth, had always wanted a child. But now they were too old.

"How can I be sure this will happen?" Zechariah asked with doubt. "We are quite old."

Luke 1

"I am one of God's angels," Gabriel answered. "God sent me to tell you this. But since you haven't believed me, you will not be able to talk until the baby is born."

Zechariah came out of the temple.

"You were in the temple a long time," his friends said. "What happened?"

But Zechariah could not talk..

 Who appeared to Zechariah?

Before long Elizabeth gave birth to a baby boy. They named him John, just as the angel commanded them.

Everyone else wanted to name the boy Zechariah after his father. But Zechariah wrote, "His name is John." Suddenly Zechariah could talk again. Then he knew God's words had come true.

Everyone said, "Wow!"

Zechariah sang:

"Praise the Lord!
God has sent a prophet to our people.
God's prophet will get us ready for the Savior!"

 When was Zechariah able to talk again?

Jesus Is Born

One day God sent the angel Gabriel to visit Mary.
Mary was a young woman who loved God very
much. Soon she was going to be married to Joseph.

"God is very pleased with you," the angel said.
"You are going to have a son. Name him Jesus. He
will be very special. He will be God's Son."

Mary was amazed. But she knew that God's
words would come true.

Luke 1–2

Several months later, Joseph and Mary had to go to a town called Bethlehem. It was almost time for the baby to be born. They needed a place to stay. But they could not find a room anywhere, so they went to a stable.

Mary had her baby. They named him Jesus. And they made a bed for him in a manger, where the animals eat.

 Where did Mary and Joseph go?

Outside of town, shepherds sat on a hillside watching their sheep. Suddenly a shining angel appeared. "Don't be afraid," the angel said. "I have wonderful news. God's Son was born today in Bethlehem. You will find him wrapped up warm and lying in a manger!"

All at once the night sky lit up with more shining angels. "Glory to God! Peace on earth!" they sang.

236

The shepherds ran to see the baby. There he was, just as the angel had said.

The shepherds told everyone they could find. They told about all they had seen and heard. And everyone who heard was amazed.

Mary and Joseph were amazed, too. Their little baby was God's own Son!

 What did the angel tell the shepherds?

A Special Visit

Some wise men came to the city of Jerusalem. They were from faraway lands. "We are looking for your new king," they said. "We saw his star in the sky. We have come to worship him."

The Jews already had a king. His name was Herod. When King Herod heard what the visitors said, he was very upset. But he kept it a secret.

Matthew 2

Herod asked the Jewish priests and teachers about this. "Where is God's chosen king to be born?" he asked.

"In Bethlehem," they said.

So Herod told the wise men, "The new king you seek is in Bethlehem. Go and find him. Then tell me where he is. I will come and worship him, too."

The wise men left.

 Who was upset about the new king?

The star led the wise men to Jesus' house. They went in and saw young Jesus. They bowed down and worshiped him. They gave him gifts made of gold and sweet-smelling spices.

But God warned them in a dream, "Herod wants to kill the child." So the wise men left the country without telling Herod where Jesus was.

Herod soon found out what the wise men had done. And he was very angry. He sent soldiers to Bethlehem. He told them to kill all the baby boys. But Jesus was not there because God had warned Joseph, too. Joseph, Mary, and Jesus had escaped to Egypt. They stayed there until Herod died.

 How did God protect Jesus?

The Boy Jesus

Jesus grew up in a town called Nazareth. He worked with Joseph in a carpenter shop. Each year he grew wiser and stronger. God was with him.

Joseph and Mary took Jesus to Jerusalem every year. They went to worship God on a special holiday called Passover. When Jesus was twelve, he and his parents went to the Passover as usual. After the holiday, they started the trip back home.

Luke 2

It was a long way to Nazareth. They walked with many friends and relatives. After a day of travel, Mary and Joseph noticed that Jesus was missing. "Have you seen Jesus?" they asked the others. But no one knew where he was.

Mary and Joseph were worried. Where could he be? They went back to Jerusalem to look for him.

 Why were Mary and Joseph worried?

They searched everywhere for Jesus. They looked for three days. Finally, they found him. He was in the temple, talking with the teachers. The teachers were amazed at how much he understood.

"We have been worried sick about you!" Mary and Joseph said.

But Jesus said, "Didn't you know I would be in my Father's house?"

Jesus was talking about God because God was Jesus' Father. But Mary and Joseph did not understand.

Jesus went back to Nazareth with his parents. He obeyed them. And as Jesus grew up, everybody liked him.

 Where did Mary and Joseph find Jesus?

Jesus and John

John was a prophet. God had given him a special message for the people: "Stop doing bad things and start obeying God. The Savior will soon be here!"

Many people listened to what John said. "What should we do?" they asked.

"If you are a thief, stop stealing. Give back what you stole. If you are mean, start being kind."

246

Matthew 3

Many people wondered who John was. "Who are you, John? Should we follow you?"

"No," John answered. "I am just a messenger. The Savior, Jesus, is almost here. He is so great that I am not even good enough to untie his sandals. When he comes, follow him!"

 What was John's message?

Then one day John saw Jesus. "Look, everybody! There's the Savior. He will take away our sins!"

Jesus walked up to John. "Please baptize me, John," Jesus said.

But John said, "Lord, YOU should baptize ME! I'm the sinner!"

"It's OK," said Jesus. "It will show everyone that I want to do God's will."

248

So John baptized Jesus in the Jordan River. A dove came down from heaven and rested on Jesus. This showed that Jesus knew God was with him.

"This is my Son," God's voice said from heaven. "I love him. I am very pleased with him."

 What did John do to Jesus?

Jesus Is Tempted

God led Jesus into the desert. For 40 days, Jesus did not eat. He was very hungry.

Satan thought, *Jesus is weak. I will get him to sin.* So Satan said to Jesus, "If you really are God's Son, prove it. Turn some rocks into bread and make food!"

But Jesus said, "The Bible says that there is more to life than food. Everyone must listen to God and obey him." So Jesus did not sin.

Matthew 4

Satan decided to try again. He took Jesus to the top of the temple. It was very high above the ground. Satan said, "If you really are God's Son, jump down. The Bible says that God will send angels to keep you safe."

"That is true," Jesus answered. "But the Bible also says that we should not test God." Jesus did not jump down. Once again, Jesus did not sin.

 What did Satan want Jesus to do?

Satan tried one more time. He took Jesus to a high mountain. He showed Jesus all the world's kingdoms. "All of this belongs to me," Satan said. "I will give you the whole world if you will worship me."

But Jesus said, "Go away, Satan! The Bible tells us to worship God. Nobody else deserves to be worshiped!"

Satan left. God sent angels to take care of Jesus.

Jesus had shown that he would not sin. He obeyed God no matter what.

 What did Jesus tell Satan?

Jesus' Friends

Jesus taught the people about God everywhere he went—in the synagogues, in the towns, and by the sea. Many people came to hear him.

One day Jesus was walking beside the Sea of Galilee. He saw some fishermen. "Follow me," he said to them. Four men dropped their nets right then. They left their fishing and followed Jesus.

Mark 1–3

Later Jesus saw a tax collector named Matthew. Matthew had tricked people out of a lot of money. "Follow me," Jesus said to him. Matthew left his job and followed Jesus.

What did Jesus say to people?

Soon many people like Matthew were following Jesus. Jesus ate meals with them and talked with them.

Some leaders said, "Why do you want to be with bad people?"

Jesus answered, "Sick people need a doctor. Bad people need to be saved from their sins. I have come to help bad people turn from their sins and obey God."

Jesus chose 12 special followers. They were called his disciples. He gave them power and sent them out to preach. Their names were Peter, Andrew, James, John, Matthew, Philip, Bartholomew, Thomas, another James, Simon-the-Zealot, Thaddeus, and Judas.

 How many disciples did Jesus choose?

A Wedding Party

One day Jesus went to a town called Cana. A friend was getting married there. Jesus and his disciples had been invited. His mother, Mary, was there, too.

"Uh-oh!" someone said. "We have run out of wine. What will we do now?" There were many guests at the wedding.

John 2

Mary went to the people serving tables. "Jesus can help," she said. "Do whatever he tells you."

Six huge clay jars stood nearby. Each one could hold enough water for 100 people. All the jars were empty.

Who told the servants to listen to Jesus?

Jesus said to the servants, "Fill the jars with water."

The servants filled all six jars with water, one by one.

Then Jesus said, "Now get a cupful from one of the jars. Serve it to the man in charge." The servants scooped out a cupful of water and brought it to the host.

"MMM!" the host said. "This is really good wine! You have saved the best for last!"

The servants were amazed. They knew the cup had been full of water. Jesus had turned the water into wine.

That was one of the first miracles Jesus ever did.

 What miracle did Jesus do?

Jesus Gets Angry

Jesus went to Jerusalem with his disciples. It was almost time for the Passover.

Jesus always went to the temple at this time of year. He loved being there.

Jesus and his disciples went into the temple. Jesus stopped. He could hardly believe what he saw.

Instead of seeing priests and teachers, Jesus saw people buying and selling things. He saw bankers making change.

Jesus got angry. He made a whip and flung it around. "Get out of here!" he yelled. "This is a place of worship, not a market! You should not be selling things in here!" He turned over the tables and made all the merchants leave.

 Why was Jesus angry?

Some of the temple leaders thought Jesus was crazy. "You have no right to do this!" they said. "Do a miracle to show us you have come from God!"

Jesus answered, "Destroy this temple, and I will rebuild it in three days."

The men sneered at him. "It took 46 years to build this temple. You can't rebuild it in three days!"

Jesus had been speaking about his body. He would die and rise from the dead three days later. But in the temple that day, no one knew what Jesus meant.

Jesus left the temple. Many people in the crowd believed he was from God. But Jesus knew that many of them would soon turn against him.

 What did the temple leaders want Jesus to do?

Fishing with Jesus

Jesus was teaching by the Sea of Galilee. Many people came to hear him. The crowd pressed around Jesus until he was right up to the water's edge.

There were two fishing boats on the shore. Jesus got into one so he could speak to the whole crowd.

Luke 5

When Jesus finished speaking, he said to Peter, "Row out to deeper water. Then throw out your nets, and you will catch some fish."

But Peter thought that it would be a waste of time. "We tried to catch fish all last night, Lord," he said. "We did not catch a single one. But since you say so, we'll try again."

What did Jesus want Peter to do?

So Peter and his helpers threw out the nets. Then they tried to pull the nets back in. But they had caught so many fish that the nets began to tear.

They needed more help, so some helpers came in the other boat. They got so many fish that the boats began to sink.

Peter and his helpers could hardly believe it. Peter bowed down to Jesus. "I should not be with you, Lord. I am a sinful man!"

Jesus said, "Don't be afraid! From now on, you will fish for people."

Peter, James, John, and the other disciples were amazed. They had never seen anyone like Jesus.

What miracle did Jesus perform?

The Man Who Could Not Walk

There was a place in Jerusalem called the Pool of Bethesda. Many sick people came there. Some were blind. Others could not walk.

One man at the pool had not been able to walk for 38 years. Jesus wanted to help him. "Would you like to get well?" Jesus asked.

John 5

"Oh yes, sir, I really would!" Then he added, "But I have no one to help me."

Jesus said, "Get up, pick up your mat, and go home!" The man then picked up his mat and walked.

What did Jesus tell the man to carry?

Some temple leaders saw the man carrying his
mat. "Hey, you can't do that!" they yelled. "It's God's
day of worship. The law says you can't work on this
day."

"But the man who healed me told me to pick up
my mat," the man said.

"WHO told you to carry your mat?" they asked.

But the man didn't know. Jesus had already left.
Jesus saw him later that day. "Now you are well,"
Jesus said. "Stop doing the bad things you used to do.
If you don't, something terrible may happen."

The man went and told the temple leaders that it
was Jesus who had healed him. They were very angry.

What made the leaders upset?

Alive Again!

One day Jesus was on his way to the town of Nain. A large crowd of people was with him. They were following him everywhere he went.

As they got closer to Nain, they saw a big group walking out of the town. All the people were crying.

What is that? Jesus' followers wondered.

Luke 7:11-17

Then they saw. The sad people were carrying a coffin. They were going out to bury someone who had died.

Jesus went up to the sad group. He saw that the dead person was a boy. The boy's mother had no other children and no husband. Now she was all alone. Jesus felt sorry for her.

 What sad sight did Jesus see?

"Don't cry," Jesus said to the woman. Jesus walked over to the coffin and touched it. The people carrying it stopped.

Jesus said, "Get up, young man!"

The dead boy in the coffin opened his eyes and got up! The people put down the coffin, and Jesus helped the boy get out.

"Here is your son," Jesus said to his mother.
The woman was so happy!

Everyone was amazed. They praised God. "God has sent a prophet to us," they said. "God has come to help his people."

The news about what Jesus had done spread everywhere.

How did the dead boy come back to life?

Caught in a Thunderstorm!

It was evening. Jesus had been teaching crowds of people all day. Now he was tired. He wanted to get away with his disciples for a while.

"Let's go to the other side of the lake," he said to them. They got in a boat and left the crowds behind.

Jesus was so tired that he lay down in the back of the boat. He put his head on a pillow, and soon he was fast asleep.

The disciples rowed along. While they were rowing, a storm started. The wind started blowing, and the rain started coming down very hard.

What did Jesus do once he got in the boat?

The waves got bigger and bigger. Soon the water was coming over the sides of the boat. The boat was about to sink. The disciples were afraid.

Jesus lay fast asleep.

"Teacher, wake up!" his disciples yelled. "Don't you care if we drown?"

Jesus got up. "Quiet!" he said to the storm. "Be still!"

All at once the storm stopped.

Then Jesus turned to his disciples. "Why were you afraid?" he said. "Don't you believe in me?"

"Wow," the disciples said. "This man is special. Even the wind and waves obey him!"

How did Jesus calm the storm?

Jesus Helps a Wild Man

Jesus and his disciples rowed their boat across the lake. When they reached the other side, they were in a different country.

As soon as Jesus stepped ashore, a wild man ran up to him. The man lived in the caves where peoples' dead bodies were buried. He wore no clothes at all. He would attack anyone who tried to come near him.

Luke 8

Jesus knew that the man had demons inside him. But Jesus was more powerful than the demons. He wanted the man to be freed from them.

The man screamed out, "What do you want with me, Jesus?" But it wasn't really the man talking. It was the demons. They knew who Jesus was, and they were afraid of him.

"Leave this poor man alone!" Jesus ordered. "Go into that herd of pigs!"

 Who did Jesus meet when he got out of the boat?

The demons went out of the man and into the
herd of pigs. The pigs rushed into the lake and
drowned.

The people tending the pigs ran back to town
and told everyone what had happened. The
townspeople came out to see for themselves.

When they got there, they were amazed. The
wild man had clothes on. He was calmly sitting by
Jesus' feet. He had been freed from the demons.

The townspeople were afraid of Jesus. "Go away," they said. Jesus got into the boat.

The healed man begged Jesus to take him along. But Jesus said, "Go back to the town. Tell EVERYONE what God has done for you!"

The man went back to the town, and Jesus left.

 How did Jesus help the wild man?

285

A Really Big Picnic

Jesus wanted to be alone for a while. He went to a spot far away from the towns and villages.

But the crowds followed him. Men, women, and children of all ages followed him. They brought sick friends and relatives so Jesus could heal them.

By evening, thousands and thousands of people had come to see Jesus.

Jesus cared for them. He healed the ones who were sick.

But the sun would be going down soon. The people needed to go home and get supper.

The disciples had an idea. "Send the crowds to the nearby villages," they said to Jesus. "That way they can get some food."

 Why were people following Jesus?

287

Jesus said, "I want YOU to give them something to eat."

The disciples said, "But we have only a boy's lunch. Five loaves of bread and two fish are not enough for all these people!"

"Bring the boy's lunch to me," said Jesus. The disciples did as he asked. He held the bread and fish in his hands and looked up to the sky. "Father," he prayed, "thank you for giving us this food."

Jesus broke the bread and fish into pieces. He handed it to his disciples. "Pass these out," he said.

The disciples did as Jesus said. Person after person took some and ate. Everyone got a big meal.

The disciples picked up the leftovers. They filled 12 baskets. Jesus had fed the entire crowd from a small boy's lunch!

 How much food was left over?

Walking on the Water

It was evening. Jesus wanted to be by himself to pray. "Go on ahead," he told his disciples. "Take your boat across the lake. I will meet you later."

The disciples got into their boat and left. Jesus went up on the mountain.

Jesus prayed until it was very late. It was the middle of the night when he finished.

Meanwhile, the disciples were trying to row the boat across the lake. But the wind was blowing the other way, and it was blowing hard. They were having a tough time rowing against it.

Then they saw him. Jesus was walking toward them on the water. When they saw him, they were scared.

Where did Jesus walk?

"Do not be afraid," Jesus said. "It is I, Jesus!"

"Lord," said Peter, "if it's really you, tell me to come to you on the water!"

"Come on!" Jesus said.

Peter got out of the boat. Step by step, he walked on the water. But then he saw the waves. He started to sink. "Help me, Lord!" he cried out.

Jesus reached out and took his arm. "You have so little faith!" Jesus said. "Why did you doubt?"

Peter and Jesus climbed into the boat. The wind died down.

All the disciples worshiped Jesus. "You really are the Son of God!" they said.

 Where did Peter walk?

Neighbor, Neighbor

Jesus taught many people. Sometimes he would say, "Be kind to others." Other times he would say, "One day a man was walking along the road . . ." and tell a story about kind and cruel people. Whenever Jesus told a story like that, he was telling a parable.

One day a smart man asked Jesus a question. "What must I do to go to heaven?" the man asked.

Jesus answered, "Love God, and love your neighbor too."

But the man didn't want to love ALL kinds of people. So he said, "Which neighbors?"

Jesus told him a parable. "A traveler was walking along the road. Robbers came, beat him up, and left him to die.

What happened to the traveler?

"Soon another man walked by. He saw the hurt man and thought, *That man needs help. But he's not my neighbor.* So he walked on by.

"A third man came along. He, too, thought, *He's not my neighbor*, and passed by without helping.

"Finally, a stranger came along. He put bandages on the hurt man's wounds. He took the man to the doctor. He paid the man's doctor bills."

Jesus finished his story and said, "Who was the hurt man's neighbor?"

"The one who helped him," the smart man answered.

"That's right," said Jesus. "Do what the helper did!"

 Which person in the parable did the right thing?

Mary and Martha

Jesus taught in village after village. One day, he and his disciples came to a village where two sisters named Mary and Martha lived. They invited Jesus and his disciples to dinner.

Luke 10

Jesus was glad for their kind offer. He said yes.
Martha went right to work. She ran here and
there doing this and doing that. She wanted everything
to be just right for her guests.

Where did Jesus and his disciples go?

As Martha worked, Jesus talked. Mary sat down near Jesus' feet to listen. She wanted to learn from Jesus.

Martha stopped. She was VERY upset. "Jesus," she said angrily, "I am doing all the work myself. Don't you care that my sister isn't helping? It's not fair! Tell her to help me!"

But Jesus answered, "Martha, Martha, don't be so upset about all the things you think you must do. Only one thing is really important. Mary is doing it by listening to me. I won't make her stop."

 What did Jesus tell Martha?

301

Jesus' Friend Dies

Lazarus lived in a town called Bethany. He was Jesus' friend. He was also Mary and Martha's brother. One day Lazarus got very sick.

Jesus and his disciples were away. Mary and Martha sent a message to Jesus. It said, "Your friend Lazarus is very sick."

Jesus said, "We will come soon." He waited two more days.

John 11

Then Lazarus died. And Jesus said, "Let us go to him."

When Jesus and his disciples got to Bethany, Mary and Martha were crying.

Mary fell down at his feet. "Lord," she said through her tears, "if you had been here, Lazarus would not have died."

What did Jesus find out while he was on a trip?

Jesus saw Mary and all the others crying. He was very sad and upset. "Where did you put the body?" he asked. Jesus began to cry.

They showed him the tomb. It was a cave with a stone in front of it. "Take away the stone," Jesus said.

At first they said, "But Lord, the body will smell awful!"

But Jesus would not change his mind.

They rolled away the stone, and Jesus said, "Lazarus, come out!"

Lazarus came out of the tomb. He was still wrapped up in graveclothes.

"Unwrap him and let him go," Jesus said. And they did. Lazarus was alive! Jesus had raised him from the dead.

 What amazing thing happened to Lazarus?

Bragging and Boasting

Jesus went to eat at the house of an important leader. Many guests were eating there. It was an honor to be at the man's house.

Jesus noticed that people tried to sit right next to the important leader. They didn't want to sit in the other seats.

Luke 14

So Jesus told the guests a parable. He said, "Suppose a friend invites you to a party. When you get there, don't sit down in the best seat. Your friend may want someone else to sit there. He may ask you to sit somewhere else. Then people will think you are not a good friend.

 Where did everyone want to sit?

307

"Instead, take the worst seat. Then your friend will want you to have a better seat. He will say, 'Don't sit there. Take a better spot.' Then you will be honored in front of everyone else.

"For everyone who brags and boasts will be put low. And everyone who acts humble will be honored."

Then Jesus spoke to the host. He said, "When you hold a party, don't just invite your rich friends. Also invite the poor and unimportant people. They can't pay you back, but God can. He will reward you in heaven."

 What happens to people who brag and boast?

The Lost Sheep

Almost everyone enjoyed listening to Jesus. Even bad people came to hear him.

But a few men didn't think Jesus should talk to bad people. They said, "This man welcomes bad people. If he were really from God, he wouldn't do that. He would only want to be around good people."

But Jesus knew they were wrong. So he told them a parable.

"Suppose you have 100 sheep and one gets lost," he said. "Do you say, 'Oh well. I've got 99 more. Who cares about one lost sheep?' No! You get worried and upset about the lost sheep. You leave the 99 and go looking for the one that is lost."

Why were some people upset with Jesus?

Everyone knew that Jesus was right. They would care very much if one sheep got lost.

"You search and search until you find the lost sheep," Jesus continued. "And as soon as you find it, you have a big party. You invite all your friends and neighbors over. You fuss over the sheep that was lost, even though you have 99 others.

"That's why I don't mind when bad people come to see me. God is very happy whenever a bad person comes back to him. I'm hoping that one of the bad people will listen to me and come back to God."

 Why did Jesus let bad people talk to him?

313

The Lost Son

Some people did not like Jesus because he ate meals with bad people and talked with them. But Jesus wanted bad people to come to God and obey him. So he told a parable to help everyone understand.

"A man had two sons," Jesus began. "The younger son said to his father, 'Give me my share of the family money!'

Luke 15

"The father didn't want his son to leave home. But he respected his son, so he gave him the money.

"The younger son went to a country far away. He spent his money on anything he wanted. But soon he had no money left. And there was no food to eat. So he went to work for a farmer feeding pigs.

 What did the younger son have to do?

"The son earned very little and had hardly any food. Finally he realized that he had been foolish. 'I will go home and ask my father to forgive me,' he said to himself.

"So he headed for home.

"The father saw him coming. He ran to his son and hugged him. He was so happy to see his son that he yelled, 'Let's have a party!'

316

"The older son got angry. 'You never gave ME a party!' he said. 'And I have always done what you said.' He would not join the party.

"But the father said, 'All I have is yours. But your brother was lost and now is found. We must celebrate!'"

 Why was the father happy?

Two Men Who Prayed

Some people thought they were better than others. Jesus told them this parable.

"Two men went to the temple to pray. One was a religious leader called a Pharisee. He obeyed God's laws and had done many good things.

"The other man was a tax collector. He had cheated many people.

"The Pharisee stood up. 'Thank you, God, that I am not like other people,' he prayed. 'I do everything that is right. I give money. I am not like that tax collector. I am a good person.'

 What kind of men went to the temple to pray?

"The tax collector prayed, too. But he was too ashamed to come all the way into the temple. He beat on his chest because he felt so ashamed. He did not even look up. He just looked down at the ground.

" 'Please have mercy on me, Lord,' he prayed. 'I am a sinner!' "

Jesus knew that the people who heard this parable prayed like the Pharisee.

Jesus said to them, "God forgave the tax collector, but he did not forgive the Pharisee. All people who admit their sins will be forgiven. But those who think they are better than others will not be forgiven."

 Why did God forgive the tax collector?

Little Children Make a Big Friend

One day some mothers brought their little children to Jesus. They wanted Jesus to bless the children.

Jesus was glad that they came. He liked children. They loved him and walked right up to him. He said hello and hugged them.

Mark 10; Luke 18

"Stop!" his disciples said. They tried to keep the mothers and their children away. "Don't bother Jesus with your little kids."

The disciples thought that they were helping Jesus. They thought Jesus was too busy to talk to children.

 Why did the disciples stop the children?

Jesus frowned at his disciples. "Let the children come to me," he said. "Do not stop them. God loves children!"

The children ran up to Jesus. They were glad that he wanted to be with them.

"Let me tell you something true," Jesus said to his disciples. "These children have become my friends just the way everyone should.

"If you want to be in God's kingdom," said Jesus, "you must love me just like these children do."

Jesus hugged the children and blessed them. This made the mothers very happy—and the children, too.

 How did Jesus feel about the children?

A Blind Man Can See

Jesus and his disciples were walking near the town of Jericho. A big crowd followed them.

Just outside the city was a beggar. He had to beg because he was blind and could not get a job. No one would care for him either.

He heard the crowd passing by and asked, "What's going on?"

"It's Jesus," someone answered.

Jesus! thought the man. He had heard about Jesus. He knew that Jesus could help him.

He took a deep breath and shouted out, "Jesus! Lord! Have mercy on me!"

"Shhh!" the people said to him. "Be quiet!"

But the man shouted again even louder.

 What did the beggar shout?

327

Jesus stopped. "Please bring that man to me," he said to the crowd.

The people near the blind man looked at him. "How about that!" they said. "Jesus wants to see you."

The man got up right away and threw down his coat. The people helped him walk to where Jesus was.

"What do you want me to do for you?" Jesus asked him.

"Lord," the blind man answered, "I want to see!" He knew that Jesus could heal him.

And Jesus was glad that the man believed. "Now you can see!" Jesus said.

All at once the man could see. He was so happy that he followed Jesus down the road.

 What happened to the blind beggar?

329

A Short Story about Zacchaeus

Jesus was visiting the town of Jericho. Crowds of people came to see him. Jesus was surrounded by people.

One man in the crowd was named Zacchaeus. He wanted to see Jesus. But he was short. He tried to see over the people's heads. But he could not.

So he ran down the street where Jesus was headed and climbed a tree.

As Jesus came down the street, he saw
Zacchaeus up in the tree.

"Zacchaeus!" Jesus called out. "Come down from
there! I must stay at your house today!"

Zacchaeus got down just as quickly as he could.
"Hello, hello," he said to Jesus. He was very glad that
Jesus had seen him.

 What did Zacchaeus do so he could see Jesus?

The people in the crowd mumbled and grumbled. "Zacchaeus is a rich, cheating tax collector," they said with anger. "Why does Jesus want to stay at his house?"

But Zacchaeus wanted to do what was right. "I will give half of what I own to the poor," he said to Jesus. "And if I cheated anybody out of anything, I will give him back four times as much."

Zacchaeus meant every word.

Jesus was very pleased. "This man has become a true believer," Jesus said. "This is the kind of person I am looking for."

And Jesus went to Zacchaeus's house.

 What made Jesus happy?

Mary's Present

Jesus had many friends in the town of Bethany. His good friends Lazarus, Martha, and Mary lived there.

One day Jesus' friends invited people to a special dinner. They wanted to honor Jesus. Martha served. Lazarus sat at Jesus' table.

All of a sudden the whole room smelled wonderful. *What's that?* everybody wondered.

Then they saw. Mary had opened a jar of perfume. She was pouring it on Jesus' feet. Then she wiped his feet with her hair.

 What did Mary do for Jesus?

But Judas, one of Jesus' disciples, thought this was a big waste. "What is she doing?" Judas asked with anger. "That perfume is worth a lot of money! We could have sold it and given the money to the poor!" Judas did not really care about helping poor people. He just wanted more money in Jesus' treasure box so he could steal it.

Jesus knew what Judas was thinking. "Leave
Mary alone," Jesus said. "God wanted this to happen.
She is getting me ready to be buried. You will always
have poor people among you. But you will not always
have me."

 Why was Judas angry?

The First Palm Sunday

Jesus said to his disciples, "Go to the next village. You will find a donkey there. Untie it and bring it to me. If anyone asks what you are doing, say, 'The Master needs it. He will bring it back.' They will know what you mean."

Jesus wanted the donkey because it was part of God's plan for him. "Your king will come to you, riding on a donkey," God's Word said.

Matthew 21; Mark 11

The disciples went and did what Jesus asked them to do. They found the donkey and brought it to him. They put their coats on it for Jesus to use as a saddle.

Jesus got on and headed for Jerusalem. His disciples followed.

What did Jesus ask his disciples to do?

As they got near the city, people came out to greet Jesus. Soon there was a big crowd. People took off their coats and laid them down, making a path for the donkey. They spread palm branches on the ground, too. They cheered loudly:

"Hosanna to our king! Blessed is he who comes in the name of the Lord! Hosanna in the highest!"

340

The whole city was buzzing with talk. People kept asking, "Who is this?"

Others would answer, "It's Jesus, the prophet from Nazareth!"

Many people did not know what to think about Jesus. But they felt sure that something important would happen soon.

 How did the crowd greet Jesus?

Dirty Feet

Jesus had been with his disciples for a long time. But he knew that he would not be with them much longer. He wanted them to know that he really loved them.

So Jesus got a towel and a bowl. He filled the bowl with water. Then he began to wash his disciples' dusty and dirty feet.

His disciples could hardly believe their eyes. When it was Peter's turn, Peter stopped him. "No, Lord!" said Peter. "You shouldn't do this. Only servants wash other people's feet."

What surprised Jesus' disciples?

Jesus said, "If you really want to be my disciples, you must let me do this."

Peter obeyed. Jesus washed Peter's feet. Then he washed everyone else's feet, too.

When Jesus was done, he sat down to teach them. "You call me Master, and that is right. But I also help you and serve you.

"That is what I want you to do for each other," Jesus said. "Do not think you are better than others. Instead, serve and help.

"Now you understand what I have done. If you do the same thing, God will bless you."

 Why did Jesus wash his disciples' feet?

Jesus' Last Supper

Jesus sat down to eat with his disciples. But he could not enjoy the meal. He was very sad and troubled.

In the middle of the meal, Jesus said, "One of you is going to help my enemies arrest me."

The disciples all started talking at once. "Not I, Lord!" some said.

"Surely not I, Lord!" said others.

Judas looked at Jesus and said, "Surely not I, Lord?"

"Yes," answered Jesus. "You."

Judas knew it was true. He had already gone to Jesus' enemies. They had paid him money. Judas was just waiting for a good time to hand him over.

Now's the time, Judas thought.

So he left.

What sad news did Jesus tell?

The other disciples stayed with Jesus.

While they were eating, Jesus took some bread. He thanked God for it. "Eat this," said Jesus, "and remember me."

The disciples took the bread and ate it.

Then Jesus took a cup. He thanked God for it, too. "Drink from this," he said. "The next time we drink together we will be in heaven with my Father."

The disciples drank from the cup that Jesus gave them.

Then they sang a hymn and went outside.

 After Judas left, what did the disciples do?

Jesus Prays

Night had come. Jesus and his disciples went to a garden called Gethsemane. Jesus often went there to pray.

"I am very, very sad and upset," Jesus told Peter, James, and John. "Stay here and watch out for trouble."

Mark 14; Luke 22

Jesus went a little farther into the garden so he could be alone. He felt very sad and lonely inside. "Father," he prayed, "you can do anything. Please don't let me suffer and die. But if you want me to, I will."

 Why did Jesus want to be alone?

Jesus went back to where Peter, James, and John were. But they had fallen asleep. "Wake up!" Jesus said. "Watch and pray so you don't get tempted."

Jesus went back to his place of prayer in the Garden. He prayed the same prayer as before.

Then Jesus went back to his friends. Once again, they were asleep. When they woke up, they were embarrassed.

"Are you STILL sleeping?" Jesus asked.

But they said nothing because they were so ashamed.

What did Jesus' disciples do while Jesus prayed?

Jesus Is Arrested

"Here comes my friend who has turned against me!" Jesus said.

His disciples looked and saw Judas walking toward them. Behind him marched a crowd of soldiers. They carried swords and clubs.

Judas walked right up to Jesus. "Teacher!" he said and greeted him like a good friend.

Mark 14; Luke 22; John 18

Judas had told the soldiers, "Arrest the man I greet like a good friend."

So they arrested Jesus.

When Jesus' disciples saw this, they asked, "Shall we attack?"

Peter drew his sword and swung. He cut off a man's ear.

 Who turned against Jesus?

"Stop!" Jesus said. "Do not do that." Jesus reached out and touched the man's ear. It healed right then and there.

"Am I a dangerous person?" Jesus asked. "I have no weapons. Why do you need weapons to capture me? You could have arrested me any time I was teaching."

The soldiers said nothing.

Suddenly Jesus' disciples were afraid. They realized that Jesus was going to be taken away.

They ran. They didn't want to be arrested too.

Then the soldiers led Jesus away.

 Who ran away?

Peter Turns His Back on Jesus

Soldiers arrested Jesus and took him away. Peter followed but did not come close. The rest of the disciples ran away.

The soldiers took Jesus to the place where his enemies were. They took him inside.

It was late at night and cold. The guards outside in the courtyard started a fire to warm themselves.

Matthew 26; Mark 14; Luke 22

Peter sat down with them.

"Hey!" a servant girl said. She looked at Peter closely. "Weren't you with Jesus?" she asked.

Peter was scared. "I do not even know him," Peter lied.

 What did Peter say about Jesus?

A little while later, someone else said, "You're one of those disciples of Jesus, aren't you?"

Again Peter denied it. "No, I am not!"

Then someone else said, "Surely this man was with Jesus. They are both from Galilee!"

Peter cursed. "I don't know what you're talking about!"

Just then a rooster crowed. And Peter remembered that Jesus had said, "Before the rooster crows, you will deny me three times."

Peter turned and left the courtyard. His heart was breaking. He thought he would never deny Jesus. But now he had.

Peter cried and cried.

 What made Peter cry?

Jesus on Trial

Jesus' enemies wanted him to die. So they put him on trial in the middle of the night. They brought in many people to tell lies about him.

Finally they asked, "Are you the Son of God?"

"Yes," Jesus answered.

They tore their clothes in anger. "That's it!" they shouted. "This man thinks he is God! Take him away!"

Matthew 26–27; Luke 23

The next morning they took Jesus to Governor Pilate. "Are you the king of the Jews?" Pilate asked Jesus.

"Yes," Jesus answered.

Pilate had the power to put people to death. But he didn't want to kill Jesus.

 What did Jesus' enemies ask him?

Pilate took Jesus outside, where there was a big
crowd. "Jesus has done nothing wrong," Governor
Pilate said. "So I am going to let him go!"

But some bad men in the crowd were telling lies
about Jesus. Soon the whole crowd believed them.
So the crowd shouted, "Don't let Jesus go! Kill him!"

"Why?" Pilate asked. "What has he done wrong?"
But they shouted even louder, "Kill him!"

Pilate didn't want to have Jesus killed. But he was very afraid of the crowd. So he ordered the soldiers to take Jesus away to be killed.

 Why did Pilate order Jesus to be killed?

Jesus Dies on the Cross

The people watching Jesus die made fun of him. "He said he could save people," they yelled. "Let's see him save himself!"

But Jesus didn't shout back. He just prayed for them. "Father, forgive them," he prayed. "They don't know what they are doing."

Matthew 27; Luke 23

One of the bad men next to Jesus joined in. "If you're the Son of God, save yourself. Save us too!"

But the other man scolded him. "We deserve to die," he said. "But this man has done nothing wrong." He asked Jesus to forgive him. And Jesus did.

 What did Jesus do when people made fun of him?

As Jesus hung on the cross, the sky got dark. Jesus' mother and his friends felt sad. But Jesus knew that they would not be sad for long.

"It is finished," Jesus finally said. "Father, I give you my spirit." And right then, Jesus died.

The ground shook with an earthquake. Inside the temple, the curtain tore in two from top to bottom. Some of God's people who were dead became alive again.

The people who saw all this were scared. Some of the soldiers said, "He really was the Son of God!"

 What happened when Jesus died?

Jesus Is Laid in the Tomb

After Jesus died, a righteous man named Joseph went to Governor Pilate. "Jesus was my friend," he said courageously. "Please let me take down the body and give it a proper burial."

Pilate was surprised. "Is he dead already?" Pilate asked the soldiers.

Mark 15; Luke 23; John 19

"The prisoner is dead, sir," a soldier answered.

"Then you have permission to take the body," Pilate said to Joseph. So Joseph went back to the hill where Jesus had died. Another man named Nicodemus went with him. They took his body down from the cross.

 Why did Joseph go to Governor Pilate?

Joseph and Nicodemus wrapped Jesus' body in special graveclothes. Then they took it to a tomb that had been cut out of the rock.

Joseph and Nicodemus gently lay Jesus' body in the tomb. Then they rolled a big stone in front of the entrance. It was hard to believe that Jesus had died.

Mary Magdalene and her friend were watching sadly as Joseph and Nicodemus buried Jesus. They all knew that Jesus loved them. And they knew he was the Son of God.

They were very sad. All they could think about was how much they would miss him. They did not expect what would happen next.

 Who buried Jesus' body?

373

Empty Tomb

Mary Magdalene and her friends wanted to bring some spices to Jesus' grave. It was a special tradition for them. So they went out Sunday morning before sunrise.

But when they got there, they could hardly believe their eyes. The stone had been rolled away from the tomb. And Jesus' body was gone!

Mary and her friends were very scared.

Matthew 28; Luke 24; John 20

All of a sudden two angels appeared. They were as bright as lightning. The women shook with fear and covered their faces.

"Do not be afraid," the angels said. "Jesus is not here. He has risen! He is alive! Go and tell his disciples!"

 What did Mary and her friends see?

375

The women ran as fast as they could. They went straight to the house where Peter, James, John, and the other disciples were staying.

They burst into the room. "Jesus has risen from the dead!" the women shouted, almost out of breath. "An angel told us and we came to tell you! We saw the empty tomb!"

Most of the disciples didn't believe it.

Peter and John ran to the tomb. They went inside
and saw the graveclothes and the strips of cloth that
had been around Jesus' head. But Jesus was not
there.

Peter and John went back to their homes. Peter
wondered, *What does it mean?*

But John thought, *Jesus is alive!*

 Who ran to the tomb?

Two Disciples

Two of Jesus' disciples were walking along the road.
A man who was traveling walked up to them.
"Hello," the traveler said. "What are you talking
about?"

The disciples looked at him sadly. "Haven't you
heard about Jesus?" they said. "He came from God.
He did many miracles. He taught us how to live. But
our leaders had him killed. That was three days ago.

"This morning, some of our friends said they saw Jesus alive. Others saw his tomb, and it was empty! But we haven't seen him."

They hung their heads.

The traveler noticed how sad the disciples looked.

 Why were Jesus' disciples sad?

The traveler was surprised. "Didn't you know that Jesus had to die and then rise again?" he said. "God told us long ago that it would happen. Men wrote it all down in the Scriptures!" The traveler explained it all.

The disciples' hearts beat fast as they listened. They were starting to understand a little better.

That night, the three men ate dinner together.

The traveler took some bread. He thanked God for it. "Eat this," he said.

Just then, the two disciples shouted, "Jesus, it's you!" But Jesus disappeared.

The disciples looked at each other with eyes as big as their plates. The traveler was Jesus! He WAS alive!

Suddenly they were very happy!

 Why were the disciples happy?

Jesus Is Alive!

Mary Magdalene and her friends had found Jesus' tomb empty. Angels had told them that Jesus was alive. Mary even said that she had SEEN Jesus.

But the disciples were afraid of Jesus' enemies. They thought, *What if Jesus' enemies come and arrest us, too?*

They locked themselves in a house.

Luke 24; John 20

"Hello, friends!" someone said.

The disciples looked. It was Jesus! They thought they were seeing a ghost.

"Why don't you believe?" Jesus asked. "It is I!" He showed them the hurt places on his hands and feet.

The disciples could hardly believe it. Jesus was alive! It seemed too good to be true.

 Why were the disciples afraid?

"Do you have anything to eat?" Jesus asked. They gave him some fish, and Jesus ate it.

"I told you that I would become alive again," Jesus said. "It's what God planned all along."

The disciples began to understand. Jesus had done what his Father sent him to do. Now everything was all right.

Thomas wasn't with them that day. His friends told him about Jesus.

But Thomas said, "I won't believe until I see Jesus and touch him."

Thomas was there when Jesus came again. "Here I am, Thomas," Jesus said.

Thomas just bowed down and said, "My Lord and my God!"

 What surprise did Thomas get?

A Special Fishing Trip

"I'm going out to fish," Peter said to his friends.

"We'll go with you," they replied. So Peter and his friends went out early in the morning. They fished for hours and hours.

But they caught nothing.

Then they heard a man call out to them. "Friends," he said from the shore, "have you caught any fish?"

John 21

The disciples did not realize that the man was Jesus. "No," they answered.

"Cast your net on the other side of the boat," Jesus called out.

Peter and his friends did what he said. They caught so many fish that they could not even pull the net into the boat.

 Who told the disciples where to fish?

All of a sudden they knew who it was. John
jumped up and shouted, "It's Jesus!"

Peter jumped into the water and swam to the
shore as fast as he could.

The others rowed the boat in. They were pulling
the net full of fish behind them. When they got to
shore, they pulled in the net, too.

Jesus had started a campfire. He was cooking bread and fish. "Bring some of the fish you have caught," he said. "Come and have breakfast with me."

They did. It was wonderful. Jesus was alive!

 What did the disciples bring to shore?

389

Jesus Goes Home

Jesus loved his disciples. They were his friends. After he became alive again, he ate with them and talked with them. He taught them just as before.

But soon it was time for Jesus to go home.

Jesus told his disciples to meet him on the Mount of Olives. It was a hill right outside the city of Jerusalem.

Matthew 28; Acts 1

When they got there, they asked, "Lord, are you going to set up your kingdom now?" They wanted him to say yes.

"No," said Jesus, "not yet. But someday I will. My Father has it all planned. Right now I must go home to heaven. But I will give you God's power. The Holy Spirit will live inside you.

What did Jesus promise his disciples?

"I have an important job for you," Jesus told them. "Tell your friends and neighbors about me. Teach them to live the way I have taught you to live. And remember that I will always be with you."

Then Jesus went up into the air. Higher and higher he rose. He went into the clouds as the disciples watched.

The disciples were sad to see Jesus go. They did not know what to say. They just stood there staring.

Then two angels appeared. "Men, why are you standing here?" they asked. "Jesus will come back someday, just the way he left!"

The disciples left the hill, amazed and glad.

 Where did Jesus go?

God Sends His Spirit

The disciples were all together. They were celebrating a special holiday called Pentecost.

All of a sudden, they heard a loud noise. It sounded like a big gust of wind. The sound filled the whole house.

They saw what looked like little flames of fire. The flames rested on each person's head.

It was God's Holy Spirit. He was coming to live inside the disciples.

Suddenly the disciples could speak many different languages.

People outside the house heard the noise. They came to look. Soon a whole crowd was standing by the door. They heard the disciples speaking in different languages.

 What happened to the disciples?

"Wow," the people said. "How did these men learn to speak this way?"

Peter knew just how to answer. "Friends," he said, "listen carefully. Jesus died and rose again." Peter then told them all about Jesus.

The people listened to every word. When Peter was done, many of them believed in Jesus.

The new believers were called Christians. They prayed together. From that day on they praised God together. And they shared all their things with each other. They lived the way that Jesus had taught his disciples to live.

And every day, more and more people believed in Jesus.

 What did the new believers do?

A Lame Man Walks Again

Peter and John went to the temple to pray. It was afternoon.

People got into the temple by going through one of the main gates. The gate was a very busy place. People came in and out all the time.

As Peter and John got to the gate, they saw a man sitting beside it. He was sitting on the ground.

Acts 3

The man could not stand or walk. He begged people to give him money as they walked by.

He looked at Peter and John. "Please," he said, "can you give me some money?"

 Who did Peter and John see at the temple gate?

Peter and John looked right at the man. "I don't have any money," Peter said. "But I will give you what I do have. In the name of Jesus, walk!"

Peter reached out and took the man's hand and helped him get up.

The man's legs suddenly became strong. He jumped up and began to walk and jump around!

"Praise God!" the man yelled. "I can walk! I can walk!" He followed Peter and John into the temple. He thanked God in a loud voice as he walked.

The people inside could hardly believe it. They ran up to Peter and John to find out more about Jesus.

 Why did the beggar praise God?

A Blinding Light

Paul was a religious teacher. He thought that Jesus was wrong. He did not know Jesus or believe in him.

Paul hated all Christians. When Christians were beaten up or killed, Paul was glad.

One day Paul decided to go to the city of Damascus. "I'll arrest all the Christians I can find," he said. He and his helpers began the long trip to Damascus.

Suddenly a bright light flashed all around. Paul fell to the ground. He was blind!

A voice spoke to him. "Paul, Paul, why are you fighting against me?"

Paul shook with fear. "Who are you?" he asked.

"I am Jesus! Now go to Damascus. A man will tell you what to do."

 Who appeared to Paul?

403

Paul obeyed Jesus.

In Damascus there was a Christian man named Ananias. God spoke to him in a dream and told him to help Paul.

"But Lord," Ananias answered, "Paul hates Christians!"

God said, "Go! I have chosen Paul to do an important job."

So Ananias went. "The Lord Jesus has sent me to make you well!" he told Paul.

Paul could see again right away. He decided once and for all to follow Jesus.

Soon Paul was telling people everywhere about Jesus. He told his friends. He told his enemies. He even told rulers and kings. He told everyone everywhere about Jesus!

 Why did Ananias go to Paul?

Cornelius and Peter

Cornelius was a Roman soldier. He was not like most Romans. He believed in God. He helped poor people and prayed often.

One day an angel came to Cornelius. "God likes the way you live," the angel told him. "Send messengers to a man named Peter."

Cornelius obeyed.

Acts 10

Peter was a Christian leader. But he did not know that God loved all people. He thought that only Jewish people could believe in Jesus.

Then God showed Peter that he was wrong. All people could believe in Jesus. Even Romans!

God also told Peter about Cornelius.

What did God show Peter?

The messengers from Cornelius came to Peter's house. "Cornelius the Roman sent us," they said. "He loves God. Please go and see him."

So Peter went. Cornelius and all his family and friends were there.

Peter spoke to them. "I used to think that I should not even go into your house. But now I know that God loves ALL people just the same!"

Then Peter told them about Jesus. "If you believe in Jesus, he will take away all your sins."

Cornelius, his family, and all his friends believed in Jesus.

They were glad that Peter had come.

And so was Peter.

What made Cornelius and Peter glad?

Singing in Jail

Paul and his helper Silas traveled all over. They told people about Jesus everywhere they went.

One day some bad people got very angry with Paul and Silas. They called the police. "These men tell people to disobey the law," they lied.

The police beat up Paul and Silas and threw them into prison.

That night, Paul and Silas had cuts and bruises all over. But they stayed up late praying and singing songs to God.

The other prisoners listened.

Suddenly the ground shook. All the prison doors opened. All the prisoners' chains fell off!

What did Paul and Silas do in prison?

411

The guard woke up. *Oh no!* he thought. *All the prisoners will escape!*

But Paul yelled, "Wait! We are all here."

The guard rushed into the cell where Paul and Silas were. "What must I do to be saved?" he asked them.

"Believe in the Lord Jesus Christ," they answered.

The guard took Paul and Silas home. He washed their cuts and gave them a big meal. Paul and Silas told his family about Jesus. All of them believed.

The next morning, the police let Paul and Silas go. Paul and Silas went to other cities. They told people everywhere the Good News about Jesus.

 What happened to Paul and Silas?

Good and Bad

One day Jesus appeared to John. "Write down everything you see," Jesus told him. "I am going to show you what will happen in the future."

John got a pen and some paper. And Jesus showed him what would happen.

"I saw God in heaven," John wrote. "The angels were praising him. Then I saw Jesus. And the angels praised him too."

Revelation 1; 5; 20

But then John saw Satan as king over the world.
Satan lied to people. He told people to do bad things.
He even hurt people. Many people listened to him.
They did what he said.

Then God stopped Satan. An angel put a chain
around him. The angel threw Satan into a big lake of
fire.

 Why did John write?

Satan had to stay in the fire forever and ever. He was never, ever allowed to hurt people or tell lies again.

Then God sat down on a great white throne. All the people in the world stood before him. Everyone who had ever lived was there. People from every country in the world were there.

And God judged each one. People who loved evil
went into the fire with Satan. And those who loved
God stayed with God.

John put down his pen. He was scared by what
he saw. But he was glad to know that good would win
over evil.

 Who will get to live in heaven with God?

Heaven

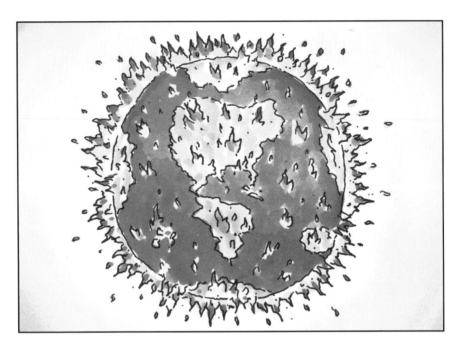

Jesus had made a promise before he left the earth. He had said to his disciples, "Someday I will come back to get you. I will take you to live where I live. And you will be with me forever and ever. It will be better and more fun than anything in the world!"

One day Jesus will keep his promise. He will make a new heaven and a new earth.

Revelation 21

God's home will be for his people. It will be for everyone who loves God. Everyone who loves what is good will love it there. Evil people will not be allowed in.

And there will be no more sadness or crying or pain in God's home. Not ever!

 What did Jesus promise the disciples?

God will have a new city, too. What a great place it will be! It will shine with the glory of God. It will be made of jewels and gold. It will be huge and beautiful.

God will be there all the time. People will be able to go right up to God and talk to him.

And there will be no night and no darkness. God's light will shine everywhere!

"I will come back soon," Jesus says. "When I come, I will look for those who believe in me. So believe in me now! Then we will get to live together in heaven!"

And John wrote, "Amen, Lord Jesus. Please come soon!"

 What will Jesus do when he comes back?

Index to Story Titles

422

Index to Best-Known Bible Stories

Index to Key Bible People